My Little Beauty Business

Sherrill Church

My Little Beauty Business

ISBN   978 0 9576265 2 2

First Edition 2013 Great Britain
Copyright ©2013 Sherrill Church

Published by Mimicks

DEDICATION

This book is dedicated to each
and every one of my students
that I have trained in college or
privately over the years –

"I wish you super success
in <u>your</u> business"!

CONTENTS

ACKNOWLEDGMENTS

To my laptop – for taking a pounding in writing this book.

To my eyesight – please forgive me.

To the many nights burning the midnight oil.

To my husband, who is my true inspiration.

…and finally, but not least, to Jane Richardson who wrote the final chapter about her journey in the beauty industry from a new therapist to a makeup artist and instructor.

CHAPTER 1

Starting Out

A Step in the Right Direction

Congratulations . . . . you've trained, you've been assessed, you've built a portfolio and you've qualified in the hair and beauty industry. But what comes next?

Business ... that's what comes next.

Regardless as to whether you're a **beauty therapist,** a **hair stylist,** a **make-up artist** or a **manicurist** the very thought of how to run a successful and profitable enterprise might fill you with fear as they didn't quite explain in detail at college just what it will take for you to become a small business owner, and actually make some really good money at it.

If this is your very first step into running a business you may feel a little unsure of your capabilities. You may be concerned about how to effectively run a business with regards to company protocol, legal administration and documenting records, action planning and just basically getting the word out there now that you are a business owner. Scary stuff maybe? Well not so. Often I hear people say that they can't run a business, they wouldn't have a clue what to do, and they have no family or friends already running an enterprise to advise them, and so on and so on with all the excuses under the sun. It's wise to remember here that running a business is actually very easy to do, very easy – it's often the case of the people running the business that make it difficult. Business doesn't need to be difficult. These people put obstacles in their own way, these people put up objections to their own success and they just don't discipline themselves when it comes down to taking consistent action in things that matter in order to make their business grow. They become stagnated and complacent with no real desire to achieve what they really can if they put their minds to it. Now I'm not saying that it's going to be an easy ride as you will need to put in a lot of time and effort and you'll have failures and successes along the way, and if this is your very first business venture you will get a great sense of self-satisfaction as you see your baby grow, no matter what route you wish to follow which could be to stay mobile or to expand into premises. This is such a great industry to be a part of. It's diverse, it's very rewarding and satisfying and it can eventually earn you a level of income you'd be quite surprised at.

Family and friends might even warn you that being self-employed is risky compared to having the comfort zone of employment. Well quite the reverse actually. Being employed you have no choice in the matter whether your job is 'safe' or not. Recently we have seen jobs in the public and private sector being taken away from hard-working, long-standing employees, who then weave their way to the job centres looking for new hope. These individuals have had their lifestyle pulled away from them without as much as a blink of an eyelid.

So being in business for yourself is far less risky as you are the master of your destiny, the creator of your Universe; you make the choices and the changes to suit your needs and your clients needs based on the economy. So no, being self-employed is far less risky than being employed as you are the decision maker on how successful you want your business to be.

To succeed at the highest level possible you will need a passionate reason to do so, remembering that what you achieve comes purely from what you believe in and what actions you decide to put in place to see your business grow. And whether you've just started out as a completely new therapist, stylist or technician or have already dabbled a bit here and there or are now a seasoned professional in the industry with many years under your belt, discovering how to reach your destiny is absolutely crucial to *your* business success.

To become truly successful, running a very profitable business is purely a matter of decision. In a nutshell – it's *you* who will decide on just how successful *you* will be. It's your decision. Whether you succeed or fail in business is entirely up to *you* and is a result of the decisions that you make on a daily basis. It will be your decision to go at it full throttle to make some serious money or it will be up to you to you make the decision to just sit back and hope and pray that your next big break (or client) will land on your lap without any effort on your part.

Why Are You in Business?

Have you sat down and really thought about why you want to have your own business. Is it because you don't want to be 'employed' by someone else anymore? Is it so that you can be in charge of your own vocation? Is it the status that could be attached to running your own show? Is it because you think you will be in a better financial situation or is it because you want to be able to pick the hours you work to suit you and your needs and your family needs?

There are so many objectives (reasons why) that you need to put in place before starting out, you need to search deep and really decide on what the main purpose is for you to enter into your own business venture. You will of course through your soul-searching come up with reasons that you may feel you will not be suited to being solely self-employed, and maybe need the continued added security of being a part-time or full-time employee as well, which is a good idea in the beginning as a new business needs time to develop and evolve in its early stages.

It will be a helpful exercise to consider the following aspects and put them into priority order as your main reasons for being a small business owner along with listing any influencing negative beliefs that you may have:

- Money – how much do you want to earn, how much do you need to earn to just scrape by, how much do you need to earn to be comfortably off and how much do you need to earn to be completely financially independent?
- Type of Work – how much of the work involved are you happy to do by yourself? Does this include all the service provision, the administration on running a business, the paperwork, the book-keeping and the very important marketing? How much of the work is satisfying or unsatisfying to you, do you need to update your skills in order to advance in any particular area?
- Working Hours – how much time are you likely to spend actually providing your service, how much time is needed for running the business and pushing it through its stages of growth, are you able

to cope with the stresses and the strains of being self-employed?

- Social Hours – how much free time are you looking to have, are you prepared to work seven days a week on your venture and always being 'open for business' having little or no time for social aspects?

- Independence and Achievement – how important is it to you to feel valued in what you do, are you able to make informed decisions quickly by yourself, are you able to set standards within your business that can be met and will you be happy to work in isolation? Are you confident in your business matters knowing that the buck stops with you?

- Family – is your partner, spouse, family and friends behind you 100% in the running of your business, if not then why not, are you and they aware that you may become blinkered towards your business and that it may take control over every other aspect of your life?

After you have drawn up your list of objectives for why you want to be in business, it will give you a clearer picture of what you are setting out to achieve along this route and it will also prove to be a very good exercise for those already in the throes of business activity.

You will discover over time that being in business for yourself can be more demanding and tougher than you ever imagined. You may worry about the security of your business, the financial flow of customer income and the dependency of the business on you as you may feel that you are irreplaceable and indispensable.

Do you know what will happen to your booked appointments if you're unable to work due to possible ill-health, maybe through a bad sprain to your hand or even a twisted ankle preventing you from driving, and what about taking a holiday – will there be strategies in place for times like these? Are you committed enough to be the chief cook and bottle washer all rolled into one.

Success Doesn't Happen Overnight

In the first few months of any new business, and sometimes for the first few years, things progress at a slow pace. Don't become too discouraged if you feel you're spending a lot of time and money in getting your business going, building up client databases, spending out on products and equipment, enrolling on industry led courses and workshops – with little or no return to show for it. This is usual practice. It's wise to remember here that if business was profitable from day one everyone would be doing it and making a fortune.

All highly successful people in our industry started at the very beginning, and this may very well be the place where you are now. Yes its daunting and scary, yes it's thrilling and exciting – but with a pre-determined desire to achieve success, however you want to measure that success, you will as long as you realise that 'Rome wasn't built in a day'. Take small baby steps, day by day, month by month, and see the outstanding results that you can achieve as your business grows right before your very eyes.

By not becoming despondent and giving up at the first hurdle you are moving in the right direction and you will have to put in to get out. Time and money spent will not be wasted as long as you continue to push forward as hard as you can, remain focused on your goals and stay dedicated and passionate towards your business venture.

What Does It Take To Be Your Own Boss?

Decisiveness and Discipline. The Double D's. For sure! In fact everything you do to do with your business and also your personal life have to have the

Double D's attached to it. Make everything you do a conscious *decision* and then add a *discipline* to it – in other words you've made a conscious decision to purchase this book and now you'll need to put a discipline in place to read it from start to finish.

You naturally discipline yourself on a daily basis in all areas of your life from getting up in the morning when the alarms goes off to eating breakfast and brushing your teeth. Think of all the other times throughout your day that you do things as a discipline, an unconscious decision, a necessity to function, without even thinking about it. You do many, many things on auto-pilot.

Get into the habit of making everything you do within your business life a Double D.

So with that in mind you'll need to *discipline* yourself to market your business effectively in order to get more clients, you'll need to *discipline* yourself to arrive at your appointments on time if you're mobile, *discipline* yourself to order more products so that you don't run out, *discipline* yourself to do the daily, weekly and monthly paperwork in order to run your business as a smooth operation. Conscious decisions will need to be made frequently and then you'll need to put disciplines in place to actually see them through.

Discipline will come into every aspect of your working day, including responding to messages that have been left on your phone or answering every email enquiry that comes in, to networking with other like-minded individuals, updating your website or blog or promotional material and always being ready to provide a first-class service that will keep your clients coming back for more.

It's all very well having many wonderful and exciting ideas for your beauty business but until you actually make a decision to act on all those wonderful and exciting ideas and put a discipline in place to see them through, your venture may just as well be only a hobby. Like I've already said, it's you that will be the chief cook and bottle washer and it's you that will be accountable for every last little thing that has to do with running a successful venture. Unfortunately there is no hierarchy, no manager or no colleague to support you and to give you a 'to do' list or to act as a sounding board or to give you a kick up the bum. Yeah sure, there are plenty of people in our industry who are eager to pass on their knowledge to the up and coming newbie's regardless as to whether that's through online tutorials, courses, chat-rooms, articles, magazines and the like – but the buck stops there as it's up to you to put their sound advice into practice and discipline yourself to see those business strategies through. Like it or not, you're on your own.

On the brighter side, however, being your own boss is a truly remarkable and exhilarating position to be in. You decide on your daily activities, whether that's servicing your clients, visiting a trade show and networking or doing the book-keeping. You decide what times to book appointments into your diary. You decide on your earning potential by setting your prices with good profit margins, or to even take part-time employment to run alongside your business to help pay the bills in the short-term. It's your business, so you'll call all the shots on just how successful it will be. Discipline yourself to really think about why you are in business and what level of success do you actually want to achieve from it.

It's Time to Kick Start Your Company

Hundreds of beauty therapists, hair stylists, make-up artists and nail technicians join our industry every year. They don't think twice about buying an endless amount of products for their kit, sometimes spending a small fortune in doing so. And with these new products and tools they practise and perfect their skills over a considerable amount of time and then they provide their service for a handful of clients . But what next? They can easily spend a couple of hundred pounds in the first few months of running their business on plenty of kit and equipment items, but most don't spend any money on investment in themselves. Yeah sure they'll buy inspirational books and magazines providing them with stimulation on the creative side ..... but what about the business side, the self-promotion, building their client list, their marketing activities, securing client relationships and actually running their business as a business and not just winging their way through. Sadly, not an influential business book to be seen on their bookshelf. Investment in knowledge is what makes the business world go round and with a whole stack-load of the latest must-have beauty, hair, make-up and nail kit is not going to be enough to succeed in this industry. Simple as that!

You, on the other hand, have taken a huge positive step in the right direction. You've bought this book because you want to know how to really run a profitable beauty venture. You want to feed your mind with the business principles and strategies that have already proven to be successful by implementing the many tactics that are ready and waiting for you over the following pages. This way you won't have to go out and re-invent the wheel as following established information is a lot faster and easier and more likely to generate success.

The businesses that I've run have all grown through investment in my knowledge – the books I've read, the people I've met, the courses I've attended. I've spent over a thousand pounds alone on business books and have quite a comprehensive and diverse collection, all of which help to feed my mind and provide the fuel and inspiration to become as successful as I possibly can. In my spare time I've usually got my head stuck into a business book of some sort, eager to learn, eager to try new ways of doing things and eager to become inspired by the greatest of entrepreneurs. This investment in my-self has been well worth it and has paid for itself time and time again. The saying is so true – 'Poor people have large televisions, and wealthy people have large libraries'!

This investment in you starts here and now. So before you settle into this book, grab yourself a notebook and pen as there will be plenty of 'Ah-ha, now that's a good idea' moments for you to write down as and when they happen.

~~~~~

CHAPTER 2

Taking Consistent Action In Key Business Areas

Let's Make Some Lists

A number one priority in running a successful business is to have plenty of ideas that you'd like to implement into your business. Those ideas, dreams, hopes and desires (or whatever you'd like to call them) need to be documented into action plans, and those actions plans usually start out as lists. So let's organise your business and make some lists.

Oh how I love lists! You can never have enough lists. I have lists for everything –shopping lists, work lists, phone call lists, books to read lists, lists of lists to write lists, and lists of jobs for the hubby and the kids to do as well. I grew up with lists, as my parents were great believers in them. Everything went on a list so you didn't (couldn't) forget. Even now I often hear my Mum say "Have you put that on your list"!

My lists initially start life on scrappy pieces of paper – well maybe not so much of the scrappy as I do use A4 sheets that have been torn into quarters and bulldog clipped together into a pad. If I didn't have these paper pads to hand strategically positioned around my home then fleeting ideas and inspirational moments would come and go as I've got a memory like a sieve and if I don't write a note or a put it on a list it's here today gone the next minute. These scribbled thoughts are then transferred into their relevant action plan folders – of which I have many.

When running any type of business, lists will be crucial to the everyday planning and administration. Without daily, weekly and monthly action plans (lists) you may find that business growth is pretty much at a standstill and not really moving forward. By keeping a focused eye on the tasks and projects in hand will help towards the planning of your future success – even if your future is simply tomorrow.

When you set out on a long road trip you may use a traditional map or a Sat-Nav as it's usual to plan your route and know what resources you'll need in advance. Business practice is no different. If you're unclear from the start about which road to follow it will take you a lot longer to get to your desired destination.

Let's start by putting your lists into priority order so that you can become more organized with your time management. You need to think about absolutely everything that you want to do and need to do in your business this week, next month and for the year ahead. But first before you can schedule in any of those business commitments you need to make a list of where all your time is actually being spent now – your priority activities on this list should include most of the following aspects:

- Time to focus on any other employment (if applicable).
- Time to get ready and prepare for work.
- Time with your spouse or partner.
- Time with your children if you have them.
- Time with your family.
- Time for grocery shopping and other shopping trips.
- Time to socialize with your friends.
- Time for housework and other domestic obligations.
- Time to exercise.
- Time to read.
- Time to relax and chill out.
- Time for short breaks and holidays.
- Time to sleep – ah!

After you've made your list to include all the priorities above and any other extra bits and bobs you may wish to add that I've not included, you'll probably find that it's already quite extensive. Next I suggest you purchase an appointment book that has time-slots in it – similar to the one you'll use for appointments, and then you can set about putting all your regular un-business related activities into it from the list you've just made above, placing each one into its relevant time-slot. Choose to do this over a 3-month time-span. Also remember to schedule in some empty time and some quality time as well. After those priority activities have been added in and of course any other employment that you may have, next add in all of your appointments and commitments that you have booked in.

Decide what else is important in your life and include it by diarising in those things of importance, making sure that they're scheduled in well in advance, like holidays and short-breaks. You must also include any other commitments and disruptions that can be a big distraction to your business life, which may be quite different from the list above, but if it's stuff you have to do, it has to go on your list! Maybe you need to think long and hard about how you could minimise any of those disruptions and turn them into effective strategies by putting them to good use.

From here you'll be able to see at a glance your available daily time and you can now start to block out hourly sections of each day that you're going to dedicate to your business growth and administration, which is paramount to your business success. You'll be able to use your appointment book as a guide to your time which will enable you to put it to much better effect. This will give you a clearer picture of how much actual time can be devoted to the marketing side of your beauty business. If it turns out that you only have 14 spare hours a week available scattered throughout the seven days then you must make sure that you use those 14 hours effectively and prioritise each week by only doing actions that are going to be business building principles that will get you moving forward. Don't waste those valuable 14 hours doing un-necessary things that will only keep your business stagnant without any growth.

If you haven't yet got yourself an appointment book you can type out some daily spreadsheets with time-slots and then start to add all your actions into the sheets over the next six-weeks. This exercise will give you a clearer picture of your time management by outlining your available hours that you have so that you can work on your business.

So now you'll have a clearer picture of your available hours that you can devote to your business growth. Each day of the week may be different, some may have only 2 spare hours a day, others may have more and some may have none. Either way you'll now be able to see what time blocks you have stretched out in front of you to fit in your business tasks and actions.

Organizing Your Lists

If you have a stack of 'to do' lists, looking at them can be a daunting prospect as everything on those lists seems to be a priority. Not so, as many tasks can be put on the back burner and re-scheduled for another day. It's all about prioritising and scheduling. You'll need some sort of order to the everyday chaos that your 'to do' lists can produce. Are your lists easy to find or are they spread over many single pieces of paper and post-it notes that are tucked away in drawers, stuck on the fridge or hidden under the bread bin, which serves as a reminder of how unorganised you may be! Your list may be a mile long or a simple one-page sheet, but either way it needs prioritising and scheduling.

Okay, so let's organise your lists. These are the ones with your ideas on and all the things that you need to do that are possibly written down onto countless pieces of paper. We'll put them into daily plans, weekly plans and monthly plans:

Daily Action Plans – You can produce daily time-sheets easily with a word processor using a table format, producing one for each day of the week. At the top of the page add a heading and a sub-heading that says:

To Do Today
Monday 3rd February – 3 Business Admin Hours

Format your table with 10 rows and 2 columns, making the left-hand column quite small and the right-hand column large. The column to the left will be for you to add time-scales into and the right-hand column will be space for the task itself. Spread your 10 lines out evenly down the page so they end up as nice large boxes.

Next print out seven daily time sheets that indicate your available time-spans and start to write in all the business tasks that you'll like to work on or achieve this coming week. It may include things like design a new leaflet, telephone a handful of previous clients or attend a networking event.

This is the time sheet system that I use which works so very well for me. On it I write everything that is a priority to do today in black pen and everything else that's not quite so important I write in blue pen. I also have space at the bottom of the page to write down in green pen some of the un-business related jobs that will also need doing like walking the dogs, nipping to the shops and doing the ironing. By doing this I'm able to see my day ahead at a glance. Ten lined boxes is usually more than enough as it's wise to remember not to be over ambitious by entering too much work to do each day or over the forthcoming week. It can be very disheartening when you get to Friday and you see how many of those business tasks are still left on your time-sheets that you didn't achieve which will end up leaving you feeling very despondent.

Once a task is achieved I then strike it through with a highlighter pen and it gives me great satisfaction if I can cross off two or three all at once!

To make your daily time sheet even more organised you could list the expected time needed for each task in the small column on the left of your table and then write each task into a specific time slot. This is being very strict and will also help you with any over-running on things that are taking up too much of your time that you can put a halt to. I have recently found a great little resource on the Internet – a stop watch that you can have displayed on the desktop of your computer which will ring out at the time you have set it to ring. So no more spending too long on time-sapping stuff and it's especially beneficial to use when you are visiting forums or checking your email inbox as those are the moments when time seems to just fly by. It can be found at http://www.online-stopwatch.com

I usually plan my daily time sheets out on a Sunday evening so that the following week is clearly laid out in a structured format and one that is easy to follow enabling me to see my week ahead at a glance. Yeah okay you may say it's a little bit on the OCD side – but hey that's just me being totally organized as usual!

Weekly Action Plans – For these action plans I have an A4 ring binder with section dividers. Each divider is labelled with specific tasks that I am currently working on. For example: website updates, email campaigns, adverts to be placed, people to be contacted, and so on and so on.

When I'm planning my working week I flick through this folder and I add anything of priority from it to my daily time-sheets. I choose the priorities first that are wealth creation; these are the ones that will reap the most benefits bringing money into my business, like adding new service information to my website. If it's not a priority or wealth creation it can wait another week or so.

With all your pending projects, tasks or whatever you choose to call them and your new business ideas stored neatly in this folder will give you a clearer picture of what you need to get through over the coming weeks. You can either tackle each one in sequence making sure that it's just right before going onto the next project or you can multi-task and have your fingers in lots of projects all at once! I hope you'll do the latter as you should try to work on several different projects all at once - simultaneously. Simultaneous action means taking action in all of the important business areas as soon as they arise and not just concentrating on one project or task over a length of time. Obviously some will take more priority over others, but doing several things at once and avoiding excuses for not taking action, greatness will emerge – even if it has an element of chaos to it. If you put all of your time and energy into one project and it became a failure (and you'll get plenty of them) you would have wasted hours, weeks even months that could have been put to better use. This does however include an aspect of pandemonium – but a great way to work as better things will materialize by working on a few projects all at once.

Unfortunately we are conditioned to take one step at a time which is okay for some tasks and aspects of life, but not always so good for the small business owner. If we did just one action at a time and saw it through to its finished result our business would grow and move forward at a snail's pace. You need to be conditioned to move with speed like the rabbit and race along with bursting energy, multi-tasking on a variety of projects all at once. If you work on three new things all at the same time rather than just working on one thing, it will triple your effectiveness and you'll get results that much faster.

Monthly Action Plans – This is the big project folder, which again has section dividers. This is where the meaty stuff goes that needs forward planning and scheduling, things that I know will take a considerable amount of time and resources.

In here will be ideas, notes and information on things like updating my customer/client database, sending out mail-shots and writing sales letters, working on new services and promotions, and setting my six-monthly marketing plan, etc. This folder is looked at intermittently and projects from it are moved into the weekly folder and from there they are then allocated space on the daily time sheets. If at any time you find that your monthly folder is bursting at the seams, then it could be time to start thinking about delegating some of your projects to family, close friends or even recruiting an assistant to help you. I've had some wonderful assistants over the years and they have been so valuable in the office taking care of the commonplace tasks which frees up my time immensely leaving me to work on the marketing side of the business and not always on the administration side of the business.

With your new ideas for business growth now safely written onto your lists in this folder they can be mulled over, built upon, tweaked and launched straight into your marketing plan. Putting ideas, tasks and projects into practice and actually doing them is so, so, so important. Remember that it's the doing that's going to make you money.

All in all, quite a comprehensive system that works most efficiently for my businesses. I have tried many things over the years and you too will eventually find a system that works well for you and your scheduled priorities, and when you do – stick to it and run with it with a vengeance.

Are You Analyzing Your Results

You may already be aware of the 80/20 principle and how it relates to everything in our life, whether that's material or immaterial. In a nutshell the formula is that 80% of your results have come from 20% of your effort? This is known at the 80/20 principle and recently I've read some great books on this subject, especially the book by Richard Koch, and to be honest I'm converted.

Judge this for yourself. Over the next working week analyse your daily time-sheets looking at all your actions and their individual time-scales. Next analyze the effectiveness of what you did by taking a highlighter pen, say a pink one and striking through every activity that added value to your business and would put money in the bank. Next take a different coloured pen, say a blue one and highlight everything that was a necessary task to do, like a trip to the wholesalers. Now drastically strike through with a yellow highlighter anything that was a complete waste of your time.

You now have some statistics =
o Pink – Do more of, again and again
o Blue – Maybe delegate to someone else
o Yellow – Stop doing

Pink is probably about 20% and Blue and Yellow are about 80%. So you need to more of the pink stuff which is going to turn into profits.

Looking at your charts you will find that only about 20% of your time is actually spent making money, which could be so much better. You need to do so much more of the 20% in order to move your business forward to its next level. Take a look at the remaining 80% and make a decision about how you can delegate these necessary tasks and how you can prevent yourself from doing totally ineffective things each and every day.

Developing Your Action Habit

There's an explicit element to success that most business owners never truly grasp. It relates to their ability to take *constant action*. Not one of any brilliant ideas that you may have will be worth a penny unless you take positive significant action. By focusing on your actions will be directly related to your income and profits. Being able to cultivate your ideas and beliefs is a crucial activity for your business growth.

Developing the action habit takes some self-control as quite often we may think that we are really busy, but if fact what we are doing is in fact a waste of time. How often at the end of your day (when you're not providing your service but working on your business) do you feel completely satisfied with all that you have accomplished? Be honest. Do you sit there in the twilight hours reflecting on your day's work and think to yourself "Well I didn't really do that much today did I, not when you consider the hours I put in"? This is called analysis paralysis. Too much thinking time and not enough doing time, faffing around so to speak. As someone once said "He who hesitates is lost". One of the biggest barriers to success is hesitation.

Most of your time may be filled up with daily drudge, unnecessary actions and highly ineffective use of the few hours that you may have. You may realise it even more so after doing the daily time sheets exercise! It's common practice to feel busy, to feel like you're achieving, but when it boils down to it and you reflect back, you're probably just (you got it) busy being busy.

Maybe you use the well known "I'm too busy excuse" to avoid taking important actions such as implementing new marketing strategies. You should set yourself a discipline to do one marketing activity every day that will lead to money in the bank – and turn that into a habit. There are probably a handful of actions that you could have taken that are probably a dozen times more effective and profitable than anything else. Focus on doing whatever it takes to remove the ineffective uses of your time and you'll see a direct impact on your growth and profits. Overcoming hesitation and taking substantial simultaneous action is both energizing and very financially rewarding.

I've also discovered that good enough is good enough. Being in the industry that we're in, we all tend to be perfectionists, which of course is very important for the service that we provide to our clients, but not so good for our business growth. It's far better to get a project going and getting it out there even if it's not quite as perfect as it could be (an unfinished website as an example) than to play around with it, tweaking it, adding to it when it was basically already good enough. Perfection can come later – launching it as 'good enough' comes first. I'd hate to add up all those lost hours I spent just playing around with things trying to make them perfect when they were already good enough. Such things spring to mind like tweaking photographs on a promotional leaflet making sure they were cropped to perfection, pixel by pixel and changing font styles and sizes just to see which one of the 30 on the short list looked better!!!! What an absolute waste of business input time. Actually I have also wasted a lot of unnecessary time on writing this book – tweaking it here, tweaking it there, generally fine-tuning it. I probably could have launched it two years earlier if I hadn't faffed around with it so much!

It's all very well having a list of actions, time sheets and project folders at the ready and having goals set and business plans in place (more on business planning in a while) if you're not going to act on them. Actions speak louder than words. You, and only you, need to make it happen! Putting things into practice and actually doing them is so important. And like I said above it's the doing that's going to make you money. Unfortunately success doesn't come knocking on your door, looking for you. It won't break your door down and insist on coming in. You have to go after it. Decide what is important in your life and include it in your time plans. Include things of importance and make sure they are scheduled into your diary – well in advance.

~~~~~~

CHAPTER 3

Working From Home

Dealing With Distractions

In most cases newly qualified beauty therapists, hair stylists and nail technicians will provide a mobile service for their clients whereby appointments are made to attend in other people's homes. You may on the other hand be fortunate enough to have the facility to devote a spare room in your home that can be converted into a salon that is fit for purpose. Regardless of the fact that your service provision may take place in other people's homes, you are still considered to be 'working from home'. There are many advantages to working from home and for starters the overheads are extremely low, and it's also very convenient having all your business assets in one place.

You may be thinking to yourself at this stage that surely running a beauty business is pretty much straight forward as there can't be that much to it. Well yes it can be like that if you only intend on doing a handful of appointments here and there, but if you want to earn serious money from your new venture then you will need to put in plenty of administration and marketing time, and by this I mean structured and planned time that you've scheduled in so that you can explore ways on how to develop and grow your business so that you are meeting your objectives on why you want to work for yourself. Time, and more importantly how you manage your time is an important foundation for your business success.

Without the luxury of the spare room, maybe you can turn a little corner of your home into 'your personal office space'. Take a look around; there must be somewhere where you can place a small desk and bookcase, someplace where you can concentrate on the job in hand to build your business. Even when running a small business you'll find that you'll have many files, folders, books, stationery, pencils, pens, rubbers and rulers that need to have their own space for storage that can be easily retrievable on a daily basis. If you are unable to dedicate an 'office-room' in your home then it is advisable to purchase some kind of bookcase with doors on, so that you can keep all your business paperwork neatly organised and in one place. You'll find that you will work a lot smarter in a more organised business setting, and your mental attitude towards it will sharpen when there is paperwork to be done as you won't have to gather together all the info you need before you even turn the computer on!

There's nothing worse than looking for a supplier invoice, your rate card or your appointments diary and having to rummage through a pile of magazines in the corner of the lounge or through all the gas and electricity bills that are stacking up on your kitchen table! Your sanity will be calmer if you know where you can lay your hands on vital information in an instant. Also, clients will lose faith in you if you have to go searching for your diary!

As your venture expands and new systems are put in place it's essential that you spend adequate time promoting, developing and improving your business in an environment that is productive for your needs. Your business is relying solely on you to make it a success and the amount of effective time and effort that requires complete concentration is an essential business building principle.

Working from home, however, can mean distractions - and plenty of them. Sometimes it can be hard to get going on your business administration and marketing because stuff keeps getting in the way. Stuff, as we'll call it, can be a major disruption to our business life. Stuff can come in all shapes and sizes and could include family and friends turning up unexpectedly, the dog barking at the postman, the kids needing your attention if you have them and the cooking and cleaning chores to be done. You can end up feeling like your banging your head against a brick wall, you can't see the wood for the trees, and instead of your workload reducing, it's escalating.

Your time is your best resource and under no circumstances should you allow anyone to steal it away from you. Most people do not place a value on their time and likewise will not value your time. Interruptions and disruptions in your daily activities will mount up minute by minute and they will eat away and prevent you from meeting your deadlines which inevitably will have to be put off.

We all know how our daily plans can somehow go adrift from what we had initially planned because of stuff happening, and it is generally stuff that needs your attention now as people unexpectedly spring things on you – some good, some bad. The clasp that you had on your time in the morning has, against your will, gone. At the end of each and every day you need to re-focus, re-organize and re-establish your priorities for the following day. This way you will be able to start the next day fresh, with a re-evaluated list.

All This Stuff Is Holding Me Back

Here is a brief list of the 'stuff' that you may encounter as a distraction in your working from home environment:

- The telephone ringing
- Family and friends visiting
- Hesitation and faffing around
- Cooking, cleaning and shopping to be done
- Maybe kids to collect from school
- The dog barking
- The double glazing guy knocking on your door
- Young siblings shouting and screaming
- The television is way too loud
- Music is blaring out

....and the list could go on and on as each and every one of us has other personal distractions to deal with in our lives.

Let's take each point that's listed above and discuss each one further in order to eliminate them as a distraction:

- The telephone ringing – a distraction yes, but a priority to answer as it could be an enquiry from a client or an appointment to be made. To avoid taking calls from family and friends at an inopportune moment make sure that their numbers are displayed on ringing, and this way you can flick onto answer-machine if necessary.

- Family and friends visiting unexpectedly – you are running a business and there is work to be done so let these people know of your 'no visit' times. You wouldn't dream of turning up at your best friend's office in the middle of the day just for a friendly chit-chat would you? Don't let them do the same to you. Unfortunately people tend to think that those who work from home are just sitting around drinking coffee and watching day-time TV. Let them know that it's not like that at all as you have priorities, schedules and above all a business to build.

- Hesitation – JFDI! (my most favourite saying). Take action in your tasks, duties and key areas that will put money straight into your bank account. Man Yana, Man Yana – always putting off until tomorrow. Stop looking at lists and tweaking them, stop tidying your desk and stop shuffling paperwork. This is all faffing around and isn't pro-active at all. We're all guilty of faffing around at some time or another and believe me, becoming too pernickety about what style and size of font to use in your leaflet isn't worth spending copious amounts of time on!

- Cooking, cleaning and shopping – this stuff can easily be delegated to another person especially if you have a partner or spouse who is supportive in your business endeavours. Maybe you could devise some sort of rota.

- Kids to collect from school if you have them – join or organise some sort of school run. Seek out the other work from home mums or dads and arrange a thorough system for home-time collection. You could even go as far as each parent takes it in turn for a week to take the kids back to theirs for a couple of hours after school. This way if there are 4 of you that means for 3 weeks out of 4 you will have an extra 30 hours of input time. Yes 30 hours. Think of what you could do with all that extra time!

- The dog barking – can be so annoying but you will find that if you break off for 20 minutes during the day to take the dog out or just to go for a brisk stroll around the block by yourself (without a dog), you'll be able to collect your thoughts and divulge in some very necessary thinking time. You'll find that you will be able to concentrate better on business matters after a little time in the fresh air. It happens to me quite often when I'm out walking Barley and Willow, my Shetland Sheepdogs, as I'm able to hear myself think better.

- The double glazing guy knocking on your door – just don't answer the door, simple as that!

- Too much noise going on is just part of family life, so enjoy it. There's no point in getting stressed-out about it, so make a decision not to worry too much about this type of distraction.

Undertaking business administration from home does have its challenges as our home comforts are all around us and it can be so very easy to be busy, being busy. So to help you through everything that will be essential in your business and daily life you need to make important decisions and set disciplines to see them through (the Double D's again) in the ever-feuding battle between Organisation vs. Disorganisation. And to become smartly organised and on top of your game in your beauty business you'll need to think about everything, and I mean everything, that your daily and weekly life throws at you and devise a structured time plan to help you through it all in your working from home environment.

Any time that you need help with self-discipline issues, you need to focus and revisit your business purposes that we discussed earlier. Is that to run your own business and to be your own boss, working from home in the hours that suit your lifestyle, being responsible for your own income and your own destiny, doing something that you'll love doing? If all of the above is important, you'll need to prioritise and kick into shape all the distracting stuff that is happening around you. Put the phone on answer-machine and leave the messy kitchen until later on in the day. It's surprising how much you can get done if you just have a clear 3-hour stretch in front of you.

To be effective in your working day you need to work to a specific time plan. You must be strict and impose these deadlines on yourself, because unfortunately no one else will do it for you. You'll also find that working against a deadline is a sure-fast way to kick yourself into action in order to accomplish the task. I know I work extremely well if I have deadlines to meet and my back is up against the wall. I suppose this fear of failing to meet the deadline pushes you to pull all stops out and to work every given hour available. The greatest invention the world has ever known is the deadline. Without it nothing would have gotten done, or been accomplished or ever achieved – a great little quote from an un-known author.

You need to claw back those wasted minutes by not allowing others to peck away at it. A 'Do Not Disturb' sign is not just for hotel rooms. You should make a practice of hanging one on your office door, kitchen door, and front door, to warn the time demons that you are stuck into a project that needs your undivided attention and you will not be available for interruptions until the sign is removed. Try having as many clocks around you as you can, as this will play an important role in your time management. You don't want to be saying, "Where did the time go". You need to know where the time went. Don't lose it and don't let anyone else steal it from under your nose.

Are You Busy Being Busy?

When you're running a home-based business you need to be organized with your time you need to think about everything that you need and want to do this week, next week, next month and for the year ahead and put some structure into your planning for the future.

Once you get going in your beauty business I challenge you to keep a diary and into it jot down only the minutes and hours that you were actually doing something pro-active to move your business forward. This doesn't include your appointments as that is your service provision which is not ultimately responsible for your business growth. That is known as working IN your business. The moments to capture are purely those that you did to work ON your business which will include marketing and promotion. Will you be surprised at your result?

Making Effective Use of Your Time

If you're running a beauty business AND you're also holding down another job to make ends meet, that can be a double nightmare. A portfolio of employment they call it these days!

Quite often I hear people complaining that they just don't have enough hours in their day, days in their week or weeks in their month to accomplish all they need to do within their business life. It doesn't have to be like that. We all have the same 24 hours and the same 7 days in our week. It's how we utilize all those collective minutes by making each and every one count in order to make them more profitable for our very own businesses.

If you already have a nine to five job during the week and provide your beauty service at the weekends as a side-line your business actions may be very limited to the amount of time you are able to spend on growth. You'll need to take each Saturday and Sunday as it comes, and if you're not out there on appointments you need to be very strict on the disruptions during those hours that you wish to use for business administration and marketing. Ask for help from your partner, if you have one, and get their support where you can. If they too can see the huge future potential that you could have with your company then they will be only too pleased to do whatever it takes to allow you quality time to spend on your business matters, in peace and quiet. It's all down to organization versus disorganization.

You know you need to put in the hours to run your business effectively, especially if you intend at some stage to give up your other job, but your current commitments elsewhere are such a drain on your time. You may have the additional responsibility of keeping home and bringing up the kids (if you have them) and sometimes it can all get too much. Oh yeah, and then there's your social life – social life, what social life, you must be joking!

You'll need to be 100% committed to your business needs or else you will always battle against time. Not enough time to do the things you want and need to do in order to push your business forward. There are never enough hours in the day, or so it may seem to you. Don't fall into that trap of being busy, being busy and stating that you haven't got enough time . . . you probably have but you just need to make better use of it!

~~~~~

CHAPTER 4

Building Your Brand

What's In a Name?

If you're just starting out in business one of the first things that you'll probably be thinking of is what to call it. During your time spent training you'll no doubt be mulling over in your mind "What shall I call my little beauty business". Before you know it you've started popping all sorts of business names around in your head. This is a usually activity – start business, so immediately decide on the name to call it.

Hopefully you're going to be in business for a long, long time and so choosing a business name is of great importance and not to be taken lightly. Don't always go with your first thought, ponder a little and bounce ideas off family members and friends. The name you choose today should be good enough to be with you next year, in 5 years and in 10 years time. Using a logo to enhance your company name can gain you greater client awareness and can be used in specific colours and font that will become consistent to your identity and in your branding.

Your business name needs to be easy to pronounce and simple to remember. You'll need as many recommendations as possible in the early stages and you don't want people to avoid this if they have problems in stating clearly who you are or even spelling it out for other people! This also needs to be considered for domain names used in websites – if you choose a business name that has a quirky spelling then you'll find that potential clients may be unable to find you because they're typing your business name into the search box in the wrong way. An easy mistake for them to make don't you think!

The same thing applies with your email address as you need to be 100% happy with it knowing that your clients will not have any difficulty using it and typing it, so don't choose a hard to write one or a hard to spell one or a hard to say one. If you spell things in an unusual manner they are very likely to get miss-spelt as people who are emailing you can make mistakes. Numbered and shortened words come to mind here, such as beauty4u or beautyforyou or beautyforu. Which one do you think could be written down incorrectly by the client? Spelling things in an unusual and peculiar manner just to be cool could result in fewer email queries and domain searches getting through. Try to avoid using your first name too as this will give the impression that you don't have much imagination and have settled for the easy 'my name' option. We're creative people, so our business name should be just as creative. Birth years in email addresses also look very unprofessional, such as yourname1975@yahoo.co.uk, this can indicate your age and the same thing applies for a numbers in email addresses like hairsalon4@yahoo.co.uk indicating that you're probably the 4th best.

If you haven't got a domain name and website running for your business using a hotmail account may be your only option, however it doesn't exactly represent a business image along with business branding does it? Once you have a domain you'll be able to have an array of email aliases with your business name included. Our domain name is mimicks.co.uk and our a main email address is info@mimicks.co.uk, plus we also have other prefixes such as sales@..., sherrill@..., ashlea@.... This way enquiries are directed to the relevant inbox. That's so much more professional than sherrill@yahoo.com don't you think?

Eventually you will have a website, if you haven't one already, and it's always a good idea to have what you actually do as part of the domain name itself. What you actually do are the 'keywords' of your business, these are the words that potential clients will search for when looking for a particular product or service. If possible use words that define your business, such as 'Oasis Beauty Treatments' or ' Face Facts Makeup Artist'. The words beauty treatments and make-up artist are keywords that will be searched for and if you have them in your website domain name you stand a much better chance of ranking higher in the search results.

The best type of business name should communicate what the business does. Take a look through the Yellow Pages and notice how many of them don't instantly tell you what the business does or offers. Try to think of an angle that you can use to speak volumes with your name which will add value to what you do. Take for instance the name 'Quintessential Hair and Beauty'. What type of image does that business name portray? Look it up in a dictionary and you'll find that it means 'the purest and the most perfect'.

Is Your Name Selling Your Story?

The best type of business name, I'm talking about any business here and not just hair and beauty, should communicate what the business does. Take a look through the Yellow Pages and notice how many of them don't instantly tell you what the business does or offers. Try to think of an angle that you can use to speak volumes with your name which will add value to what you do.

You may have some unique element about you or your service that you can encapsulate in your business name. It should create a 'good-feeling' to your clients, give a clue to your image, and be as original as possible to any other business name regardless of the industry. I often ponder over everyday sayings and then in my head I try to match them up to a business category, any business category. It's such a fun thing to do, probably silly but you should have a go at it. An example of this is the business that sells bathroom design called 'Just Add Water'. What a great business name! A friend of ours is a builder and his company is called 'Brickin' It'! That one's not easily forgotten either.

Before deciding on your choice of business name you should research through the Internet to check if the name is available and hasn't been used elsewhere, preferably on a Global scale. Check out Companies House for registered business names and the Information Commissioners Office for names that are trademarked. Should you wish to register your name as a Trade Mark then this is easily done and it's not too expensive to do, and it will safeguard you against any other person or business using your name. Trade Marks can be registered on a National or International basis, and this will allow you to use the appropriate symbol against your company name.

Your Unique Selling Proposition

What is going to make you as a beauty therapist, hair stylist or nail technician stand out from the rest? Why are you so different? What's so unique about you? Your unique selling proposition, that's what. You may have heard other successful business owners talking about their USP.

A unique selling proposition (or unique selling point) can be anything from one word to a sentence or paragraph that you can use in your marketing that completely summarises what you and your business stands for. All the big boys use one, and they can also be referred to as tag-lines or strap-lines. Think about the most popular ones that have become household sayings over the years, such as:

'Probably the best in the world' - A well know lager
'Lovin It' - A burger
'Simples' - A price comparison website
'Holidays are coming' - A fizzy drink
'Because you're worth it' - A product range

Longer USP's with more substance outlining a promise made to the customer go along the lines of: 'Fresh hot pizza delivered in 30 minutes or less, guaranteed'. The above USP has three messages rolled into one; what's being sold, how quickly you can get it, and a guarantee to confirm that if it's not hot or delivered within 30 minutes or under, you are likely to get it for free! That USP made Tom Monaghan from Dominoes Pizza a multimillionaire and helped to dominate control in the pizza industry, not only in the USA but also the World, from his first small single outlet. His USP not only incorporates the benefits of a fast delivery service but it also has the added benefit of a guarantee!

Unique selling propositions like that are classics and will stand the test of time and there's no reason at all that you too can't come up with an amazing strapline to summarize your business benefits.

Your USP can be based on any element of your business – the service, the product, your company policy, business name or even location – anything that you desire, but it's most important mission is to relay the benefits of what you are about or what you can do for your client. Come up with an influential claim that is yours and only yours on the basis of what you do. A good USP can take months, even years, to come up with so it's not something that needs to be rushed and set in stone with your first thoughts on the matter. Take time to ponder what other businesses have used and try to uncover why they have used it. Think about the services and products that you use on a regular basis and ask yourself 'Does my loyalty to that company have anything to do with their USP, is it delivering an emotion or benefit that is close to my heart'. Become USP receptive and ask questions to yourself about every business, product and service that you happen upon on a daily basis in order to bring to light your very own selling proposition.

~~~~~

CHAPTER 5

Putting Systems In Place

Business Administration

The success of your business doesn't just happen; you must plan for it to happen by putting thorough systems into place.

Maybe by now you have provided a few services to your clients and are now looking towards getting a good system together regarding your paperwork. To run a business effectively, a dependable business administration system needs to be put in place. For without some kind of structure to not only your appointment structure but also your administration, you could easily find yourself becoming overwhelmed with it all and on the other hand becoming despondent and losing the passion that you once had when starting out.

It can be very easy to tie yourself up completely in the running of your business by sacrificing your health, family and sanity. In order for you to own the business and for it not to own you, you will need to develop effective systems that will deliver foreseeable results from routine use. A business system is relatively easy to put into place from start-up as it will be a step by step process, and each building block that you put in place will form a structure in which to build the next block from.

All businesses start out with nothing apart from the first seedling, the very first idea. Over time as the business grows so does the ideas regarding the systems on how the business will operate which have been tried and tested through trial and error. The big National branded companies were also once there right at the beginning as a start-up company, like we all were, and have spent many years perfecting their business format. They too once went out and purchased their first batch of business cards, designed their first letterhead and put together a basic brochure in which to woo and attract their clients or customers. You will be doing the same as they did.

All your paper-based sales material should be consistent in image, which includes colour, typeface and logo, if you have one. People can become easily confused about your image if it's all over the place with one style of writing for this, a different colour for that and varying styles of a logo. Think long and hard about your image and how you wish to portray your business and reflect your style, and keep it consistent in all areas at all times. Before you rush off out there to have any of your sales material printed, it's a good idea to have a friend proof read your item in case of any typos or grammar issues that may be flagged up.

So to start with the real basics of a good administration system, which will include your sales material, let's start with the simplest of all humble essentials:

Business Cards

This is without a doubt one of the first investments you need to make just at the onset of your beauty venture. No matter how large or small you anticipate your growth within the industry, your business card will be an essential element for your future growth.

You will encounter many opportunities to hand your card to prospective clients, to use as a referral or to take with you when meeting suppliers or networking. Without one in your purse, wallet or handbag is an admission that you are not as serious as you thought you were about your business and that lack of passion will be felt by others. 'Hey, can I have your business card' – 'Ooops sorry, haven't got one on me'. Oh dear!

If you are designing your own business card you will find that print-shops on the Internet will display the image sizes, format and resolution that you can follow to produce your own. Some even provide templates for you to use – but these can be pretty basic. You may be lucky enough to know someone in graphic design who will be happy for you to commission them for your project.

After you're business card has been designed and is ready to go to print you can again search the web where you'll find an abundant of printers listed on the Internet that you can choose from, quotes tend to be instant as well, and prices range from free to very cheap to very expensive. A word of warning here though – do be wary of the free type as these sometimes require that you have the name of the print company printed on the reverse of your card. This can de-value your business and you could be considered a cheap-skate for choosing freebies which will reflect on the quality of the service that you provide.

In the beginning its best not to order a run of too many cards as over the first couple of months of handing them out to prospective clients you are bound to find things that you are not quite happy with, and you will want to make changes for improvement, which you can do prior to the next run of them. Small print runs of say fifty are a good start.

On receipt of you business card, be sure to always have a small batch about your person, in your kit box or in your car. You never ever know when an opportunity will present itself, and there's nothing worse than promoting yourself to someone, then rummaging around in your handbag, and not having something tangible to give to the other person to remember you by! I always make a point of sending a business card out with generally any letter or other document I send out in the post. People are likely to keep a business card that has been sent to them as it's easy for them to pop it into their purse, wallet or business card holder – and hey presto it's easily retrievable should the moment arise that they are able to recommend you. Don't miss a trick for promotion.

Letterheads

With your business card now in place, it's time to create your letterhead. This will have the same branding image as above and again only a small quantity will need to be purchased in the beginning.

Your letterhead will be used for mailing out to clients with details of any up and coming promotions and any other personal correspondence you may wish to send to them. Incidentally if you intend on sending out direct-mail you should always make an effort to find out the name of the person that you're contacting, especially in a business capacity as no-one likes to receive a letter headed 'Dear Sir/Madam' or at worst 'To Whom it May Concern'! Get personal and get noticed.

You will also use your letterhead to contact trade suppliers and to contact your bank, your accountant, the Inland Revenue and possibly your local Council. A letterhead creates a professional image and can also double up as the document you use to print appointment reminders, invoices, receipts and likewise.

Even a small run of a hundred will be worthwhile in the beginning, but don't forget that you will pay a more premium price for small quantities. If you're designing and printing your own letterheads you can give them a more professional feel to them by using a top quality paper like Conqueror.

Leaflets

Your leaflet needs to give a *brief* outline of the type of beauty service that you offer, a sort of taster or menu if you like, from which the client can become interested to find out more about. The leaflet, whether single-sided or double-sided doesn't need to go into specific detail, but just enough information to whet the clients appetite, enough for them to seek you out further and even look at you website if you have one for a comprehensive account of what you do.

Leaflets are similar to business cards but bigger and with additional information, and should be used in the same way – ready to be produced to a prospective client in any given moment. They are also a good tool for mail-shots, or to leave on counters at complimentary businesses (gyms and health clubs as an example) or to place as a loose leaf inside the local community directory or newspaper.

Your leaflets can change their appearance as often as you see fit, maybe when you launch a new service to promote a holiday theme like Summer or Christmas. It is also quite usual to have a couple of different styles of leaflets going at the same time.

Less is more as far as your leaflet is concerned, so try not to over-cram it with too much information, ridiculously small print and irrelevant particulars. Don't be afraid of 'white space' as this can give the impression of calmness and clarity to what you are offering – however too much white space can also be a wasted opportunity for your business promotion! So get the balance right.

Brochures

The business brochure is probably one of the hardest and most complicated of all the sales material to produce. Your brochure can make or break you and can speak volumes about your business and the class of service that you provide.

The first consideration you will need to take is what size and style to produce it in and this can be tricky as there is so much to choose from. Styles come in all shapes and sizes from single-fold to bi-fold, from tri-fold to gate-fold, and from A4, A5 and A6 multi-page brochures in a landscape or portrait manner. Phew – such a choice!

Once you've decided on your budget and on the style of brochure the next job is to think about what you would like to include in it. Just write a brainstormed list to start with (or have yourself a blue-sky moment as they say now)! Next make a draft copy of the brochure size and its layout, being sure to put the creases in the correct place if you intend on having a folded one.

Then, in pencil, start transferring the information from your list onto the draft copy positioning each item as you see fit. If you have many services to promote it's best to place them into similar groups for easier reading as you want your prospective client to feel comfortable with the layout and not have to search for crucial information as their reading experience will need to flow. At this stage it's important to place your business name and logo in a prominent position, and all the contact information necessary as you don't want to have to squeeze this in as an after-thought.

If you are adept at using a graphics editor such as Photoshop or Fireworks you may wish to also plan it out there as you can easily build layers which you can drag and drop into their relevant place. Printing your draft copy out will also give you a greater understanding of how your finished item will look.

Areas to take into consideration, when planning out your brochure, is firstly the layout as above, and secondly the text (copy) that you will be adding. Do you want to provide comprehensive explanations on each of your services or just bulleted lists with a brief description? Either way, make sure that it relates the benefits to the customer, which is discussed in more detail in a subsequent chapter.

A bad example of this would be:
- Manicure – including hand massage, polish and top coat [timescale and price].

A good example of this would be:
- Revitalizing Manicure – your hands encounter many strains and stresses during the day and they will greatly benefit from an invigorating massage which will increase circulation and nourishment to your arms, hands and nails by using our/my specially blended creams. Your manicure is completed with a coloured polish of your choice and set with a hard-wearing barrier for those hard-working hands [timescale and price].

All of the copy used throughout your brochure should be client focused by using the words 'You' and 'Your' to communicate the benefits of the service and what it will do for them. This makes it more personal to them and as they read it will make them feel that's it's all been written about them for them. Great psychology at its best! This is not the place for your own ego boost on how professional you are, how brilliant your beauty treatments are or how many years you've been established. The brochure is all about the client and what they want, need or desire, not you.

Before you have a complete run of brochures printed, it is advisable to see a sample copy prior to placing a confirmed order as this could bring to light any spelling or grammar mistakes, any misalignment of text or images and any colour considerations that may need to be altered. It's imperative that you do use a spell checker and also a high resolution for any photographs used, as your print-shop will unlikely check these things out for you and may not be held accountable.

You will be exited and apprehensive for your first batch to arrive, and when it does, then proudly hand them out to anyone and everyone for maximum exposure!

Complimentary Slips

A complimentary slip is not a necessity; however it's a nice thing to have. Based upon similar styles to your letterhead, you can use your complimentary slip to send hand-written notes to clients or suppliers, and also use as a packing slip if sending products or freebies out in the post.

Invoices

At the moment you may feel that it's not essential for you to use invoices but there may come a time when you need to invoice clients for services rendered or to send out products if you have a retail range to sell.

Nothing looks more professional than a quality formatted invoice. These days it is not necessary to purchase expensive invoice pads that have been custom designed by your print-shop, as you can quite easily prepare and produce invoices from your own computer and colour printer.

Your invoice will need to have all your company details printed on at the top, which will include business name and address, telephone and mobile number, email address and website. You'll also need to include a company registration number if you are a Limited company and a VAT number if you are VAT registered. Incidentally – VAT registration is only applicable when your turnover reaches a certain level. Your invoices need to be numbered in sequential order from the very first time you issue one and this numbering system must be consistent throughout your business life.

As an invoice is a request for payment from a client, customer or supplier, etc, it should also indicate somewhere about your preferred payment methods. If accepting cheques then the name in which the cheque is to be made payable too needs to be clearly shown, and if you accept BACS payments then the details of your business bank account must also be provided – sort code and account number. Incidentally you'll need a business bank account to run your business. Using a personal account to pay cheques into from your clients will lose credibility.

An invoice can either be just a typed-out document outlining the services or products rendered or it can be produced in a table format which will enable you to list multiple items. You don't even have to start from scratch when designing your invoice as there are plenty of templates to be found on the Internet.

When printing out your invoice it is essential to also print a duplicate copy that you will need to keep for your book-keeping records which you'll be handling over to your accountant. If you intend to have accounts with any companies whereby they pay on terms (14, 21, 30 days, etc) then it will be necessary to send them an invoice outlining the service particulars and costs. Your duplicate copy that you will keep on file will serve as a reminder to you regarding outstanding debts that are owed.

Not all small hair and beauty businesses have the need for invoicing as most stylists and therapists collect payment on completion of their service. However, if you intend to build accounts with clients whereby they can pay at the end of the month say, then sending them an invoice will not only provide them with details of their account, but will also serve as a reminder to you regarding outstanding debts that are owed to you.

Receipts

On collecting a cash or cheque payment from a client on the day your beauty treatment has been provided, you can use a receipt pad for this purpose. It is not necessary to print your own pads as these little booklets can be purchased from most good stationery shops. They are quite self-explanatory and all that needs to be documented is the date, the client's name (and possibly address), the treatment provided and the fee paid to you.

Again the receipt pad will need to be in a numbered order and the duplicate copy must be kept for your records. Pads usually come in duplicate sheets of a hundred and for your records you can prefix the batch of numbers with A, B, C, etc. For example A1 through to A100, and the next receipt pad purchased would be B1 through to B100, and so on and so on. This will assign a specific 'folio' number for each pad that you purchase that will be easily recognisable to you and your accountant when organising your bookkeeping for that financial year.

Your Appointments Diary

Your appointments diary is the lifeline of all your business activities and should be easily retrievable at a moment's notice. There is nothing worse than having a prospective client on the phone wishing to make an appointment and all of a sudden your diary has gone 'walkies'. Over the years I have used many different styles and types of booking-in systems and have gone from large day-per-page diaries to those little miniscule pocket ones (which I must add were an absolute waste of time).

I find that the 'week at a glance' is by far the best choice, as when an enquiry comes in I can open the diary at the relevant week and can see immediately what my availability is. I use different coloured pens to book in different types of appointments or commitments, and in pencil I include any provisional arrangements that have also been made. Never miss an opportunity for future business – take your appointments diary with you wherever you go as you never know who is going to ask if you're available on a particular date.

So with the few business basics as listed above the next step is to write a handy script to follow for when your prospective client phones to make an enquiry.

Pre Written Scripts

If you are new to business it can be quite a daunting prospect when the phone rings and your intuition says that it's an enquiry from a client. By having a pre-written script close to the phone you need never have to worry about what to say to the person on the other end of the line.

In order to write a script it is necessary to go through the process of role-play, whereby you are the client and you are also yourself. Take a sheet of paper and start to brainstorm a conversation on how the enquiry might go.

Start off by scripting how you would like to answer the phone call. Remember that you are in business and it can be quite off-putting if you just pick-up and say

'Hello'. Speaking out loud to yourself, try saying "Hello [and your name] speaking", or perhaps try saying "Hello [and your business name]". This time say "Good Morning, [your name], how can I help you". Now try the above again but this time say it with a big smile, it will almost always sound different coming from a cheery disposition.

Next, the prospective client will usually say "Oh Hi, yeah I'm just phoning up about ....." and she will speak a sentence or so either about her requirements or about an advert she's seen, or for the further information outlined in your brochure. Listen with care at this point, don't interrupt and only speak when she has stopped talking. If she gives you her name, make a point of writing it down immediately and you can then use it during the conversation with her and she will be most impressed that you have remembered it.

Your next job is to confidently answer her query with as much information as possible. During this stage you should ask her open-ended questions in order to gain more information on her requirements. Each time the prospective client speaks; you must stop talking and listen to what she has to say. Their part of the conversation is the most important aspect so try to avoid butting in inappropriately. This, however, can sometimes be difficult to do as we just want to provide them with as much information about our business as possible as our passion for our industry takes over.

After you have given the client the necessary details which might also include the price, it is time to close the sale and make the appointment. During the phone call you would have located your diary and be in a position to offer her the date and time. Not all enquiries however will turn to a committed appointment and if you feel that you are losing her or she states that she'd like to go away and think about it ask if you can take her email address so that you can forward her a quotation outlining the details of the service she has enquired about and offer to send her your special report/newsletter (a lot more on that later). By offering her something free and something of value should make a good impression about who you are and what your business is all about. This client will now be intrigued, so act upon sending her this free information as soon as you can, preferably within a couple of hours.

Should your client make a booking with you, this part of the script will include taking details of the service required along with her full name and address. It is also important to take a contact telephone number and I always make a point of taking both a land-line and a mobile number and of course an email address. Thank her very much for her booking and let her know that you look forward to meeting her soon.

Other scripts that you might like to write are for telephoning your clients about promotions and special offers, or new service launches.

Storing Your Business Records

With your bookshelf at the ready that we discussed in an earlier chapter you will now need to fill it with files and folders of all sorts and if you're anything like me, I have to have all my files of sort in a particular colour and style (OCD or what)!

Below is a list of all the types of files and folders that I have at the ready to place the relevant paperwork into:

• Client Information
 Consultation sheets, client record cards, addresses, email and telephone databases. Data protection could apply here so contact the Information Commissioners Office (ICO). In here you can also keep internet release forms of any client photos taken and allergy declaration forms.

- Invoice Folder
  Invoices awaiting payment
- Training Folder
  Any information regarding forthcoming
  courses that you'd like to attend to enhance
  your skills, new product launches that you may
  wish to invest in and details of forthcoming
  trade shows and maybe a list of all business
  books you'd like to read.
- Products Folder
  Current information about the products that
  you use including ingredient lists, wholesale
  price-lists and suppliers details, along with
  website information for other product
  suppliers.
- Health and Safety Folder
  To store all information related to health and
  safety, codes of practice, risk assessments, patch
  test forms, method statements, insurances, local
  bye-law information, affiliations and trade
  memberships.
- Swipe Files
  For absolutely anything that you have taken
  from other sources that you can use for
  inspiration in your advert writing, brochure
  design layouts, business colour schemes, ideas,
  tips and tricks. As the name implies – it's
  something that you have swiped from

somewhere else to help you at a later date and could include photographs, images, wordings for copy-writing and even your competitor's leaflets, etc.

The next batch of folders contains information that I will be going through with you in the legal requirements chapter:

- Book Keeping Folder(s)
  This can be quite extensive as you will need income folders and outgoings folders, along with bank statements, etc.
- Action Planning Folder(s)
  All your lists for daily to do's, weekly to do's and monthly to do's, time management plans and self analysis forecasts.
- Client Target Market Folder
  Anything and everything to do with your target market and who your client is, surveys and testimonials.
- Business Planning Folder
  For your objective master plans, cash-flow plans and finance plans.

As well as the customary files and folders kept on your book-shelf you will also need to allocate a specific folder on your computer or laptop solely for your business venture. This folder can then be split into many individual folders to store documents such as invoices, scripts, information forms, emails to send, databases and adverts, etc. As well as keeping this type of information stored on your computer you should also save it to a memory stick or external hard-drive as a back-up and it's also worth printing out hard-copies of all of these documents as well and then storing this information in a folder named General Admin.

Systems deliver expected and reliable results. Systems will give you more control over your business, better management of your time, less pressure and a better relationship with your clients. Always make every effort to put a system in place, no matter how small or insignificant it may seem, as they can absolutely transform your business and your working practices.

Don't let your business own you – you need to take control and own it!

~~~~~~~

CHAPTER 6

Legal Requirements

The Inland Revenue

Being self-employed and running your own beauty business is not as hard as you may think with regards to keeping on the right side of the law and keeping up with the paperwork – as long as you put systems in place from the onset which will be briefly explained in this chapter. I would, however, also seek to take further advice from an accountant or other business advisor as there are additional requirements that you will need to be aware of when running a small business. So what are the basic requirements that you need to follow? Written here is just a brief explanation of what is needed to get you going and to keep you on the right side of the law.

As soon as you set up in business for yourself it's a good idea to notify the Inland Revenue as soon as possible, regardless as to whether you have made your first sale or not.

By doing so they will have all the information needed about you and your business venture for when the times comes that you start taking money from a paid service from a friend or client. The moment cash, cheque or card exchanges hand – that's the moment you're in business, no matter whether it's for a fiver from your best friend or for a tenner from the lady down the road. You're in business. If you delay registering, you may have to pay an initial penalty fee. You'll also have to pay further penalties if payments of tax become due and have not yet been met.

When you become self-employed you must register for Income Tax and National Insurance purposes with HM Revenue & Customs. If you are in a partnership, each of the partners must also register separately.

The information that they require will be:

- Name
- Address
- National Insurance Number
- Date of Birth
- Telephone Number
- Email address
- Date Self-Employment Commenced
- Nature of Your Business
- Business Address – if different from above
- Business Telephone Number – if different from above
- The Business's Unique Tax Reference if you are joining an existing partnership and the business partners details

Make sure you have all of this information to hand if registering online as you can't save the details and return at a later date once you have started to complete the online form. You will then be issued with your very own UTR code (Unique Tax Reference) which you'll use for all your self-employed dealings throughout your business life.

You won't need to register for VAT until your taxable turnover reaches a certain limit, and there's plenty of advice available when it does from the Inland Revenue website. HMRC also provides free workshops and events that help new and expanding businesses progress through tax and VAT requirements.

For further information regarding self-employment, income tax and national insurance contributions, visit their website at www.hmrc.gov.uk

Basic Book Keeping

Being self-employed requires you to keep a record of accounts which isn't half as scary as you may think, as all it takes in the beginning is a couple of spreadsheets that you can easily format in Excel, or as a table format in MS Word. Think of your book keeping as having two baskets – one which you will fill with all records of money going out, and the other you will fill with all records of money coming in (which hopefully should be the bigger one of the two)!

Let's now make a list of everything you're going to put into basket number one, the things going out:

Expenses – also known as Business Outgoings
Expenditure receipts are items that you have spent money on to run your business and can include things such as:

- Product supplies – all materials needed to provide your services.
- Tools and equipment – items purchased to enhance the application of your services.
- Rents and commissions – fees paid to attend any events as a trader such as wedding fairs and beauty shows.
- Reference books and magazines to keep you up-to-date with current industry trends.
- Uniform that you have purchased to keep within the professional standards of the industry.
- Stationary and sundry items purchased to help put business administration systems in place.
- Printing costs – all the materials needed for your sales literature and the promotion of your business such as brochures and business cards.

- Advertising – placed in magazines, newspapers and the like.
- Online advertising which will include your domain purchase, website costs, hosting package and any Adwords campaigns.
- Office equipment such as computer, printer, software, desk, chair and bookcase.
- Postage spent on stamps for communication to your clients and suppliers and courier charges for sending out packages.
- Professional fees to your accountant, business advisor and for any professional training courses undertaken.
- Motor expenses – this would include repair costs and road tax and the fuel and oil that are needed to run your car on a daily basis to get to and from your appointments, suppliers, etc. Log book, valuation, emission, and purchase record regarding the vehicle must also be kept.
- Telephone – a proportion of the bill from your land-line and mobile phone will be tax deductible, so keep the complete invoice and your accountant will be able to apportion it for you based on usage.
- Overheads – this will include any additional council tax or business rates that you pay on your home as a business premise.
- Insurance and licenses – your public liability and product liability premiums as well as any charges

made from your local council regarding trading bye-laws.

- Repairs and servicing of any of your equipment including electrical PAT testing.
- Equipment hire – this could include things such as compressors, gas cylinders or fire extinguishers.
- Drawings made by you from the business bank for your personal wages and expenses.
- Bank charges that your bank will produce from your business account and any credit card fees if you have a card payment facility set up. This also includes any PayPal or Google Checkout transaction fees.
- Rental and rates overheads if you have business premises or a shop/salon.

Your expense records will come from your bank statements, your company cheque book and any credit card statements. All cash expenses must also be recorded by documenting small purchase receipts.

As you can see it is quite a comprehensive list. If in doubt of what receipts and sales invoices to keep – then keep them all and your accountant will be able to advise you accordingly at the end of your financial year. Oh incidentally – your financial year runs from the date that you started and registered your business and doesn't necessarily mean from January through to

December as it could very well be from September 23rd through to September 22nd the following year, or whatever time you notified the Inland Revenue of your business start-up.

Income – also known as 'Money in the Bank'
Your income will come from sources such as:

- Services provided
- Products sold for retail purposes
- Any training provision that you are in a position to give to others for a fee being paid
- Any pieces of equipment used in the business that you sell on as second-hand
- Any other miscellaneous income that is linked to the business
- Interest paid to your business bank account by your bank

Your income records will come from your invoices that you raise to your customers and from the receipt books that you keep when you have been paid for services rendered. All income in cash payments must also be documented. Other records of income are your bank statements and your paying-in book.

Record Keeping

As well as your cheque book, paying-in book, bank and credit card statements you should also keep records of petty cash spent, an inventory of stock and working products in hand, a list of capital equipment that you have purchased and any details of money taken out from the account for your own personal and private use, along with details of any personal money invested into the business.

Organising Your Accounts

Basically – three lever-arch folders with dividers is all that you will need.

EXPENSES FOLDER:

In your first lever-arch folder, place into it 12 monthly section dividers. Under each month you will file all the invoices and receipts that you have collected from basket one, in descending date order for the month. At the beginning of each month, put in a plastic wallet and in here you can store all the little petty cash receipts that you're unable to hole-punch.

On the receipts and invoices that you are storing in here, write in red pen across the top of the bill how much the invoice was for and whether it was paid by cash, cheque or card. If it was paid by cheque you will also need to write the cheque number on here as well.

File information in this folder on a daily basis as a discipline if you can or at least weekly and keep this system going for each month. This makes up your expenses folder. If done on a regular basis it will grow easily and you won't need to spend countless hours trying to sort it all out at the end of your financial year.

INCOME FOLDER:

Your second lever-arch folder will be organised on the same principle as the first, with similar 12 monthly dividers, however this time it will contain the invoices and receipts from income earned through services rendered and products sold. Again, file the information in this folder on a regular basis and keep this system going for each month. This makes up your income folder.

ACCOUNTS FOLDER:

In your third lever-arch file, place in 5 section dividers and label then with the following titles: Expenses,

Income, Statements, Drawings (wages), and Miscellaneous documents.

In the Expenses section you will file the 12 spreadsheets for the year's expense accounts (more about these in a moment) and in the Income section you will file the spreadsheets for the year's income accounts.

Your bank statements will be stored in the next section and will include those from the bank, from your credit card company, from PayPal and any building society that you may hold. A drawings and wages spreadsheet will follow in the next section and in the last of the section dividers you can keep any additional miscellaneous information that your accountant may need, such as any P45's from other employment, any correspondence from the Inland Revenue, stock control sheets, equipment resource information and vehicle details. This makes up your accounts folder.

Account Spreadsheets

An Excel spreadsheet is the easiest way to record your accounts on your computer until you progress to using specific software for the task such as Sage Instant Accounts.

Make it a discipline to update your spreadsheets on a weekly basis by entering the information that you have stored in your Expenses folder and your Income folder, in order to keep on top of it all. If you fail to do this you may find it can become overwhelming if you have many entries to post and your memory doesn't serve you well in remembering all the necessary information. For an even more effective method you could even do it on a daily basis and that way it shouldn't take too long. As you reach the end of each month and all entries have been posted you can print off a copy to store in your Accounts folder. Always make a back-up on saving the changes on your computer so that you have a failsafe system in place.

At the end of your financial year and prior to the self-assessment deadline of January 31st – you can hand over your three very organised folders to your accountant for revision, and I'm sure he or she will be very impressed with the organisation of your paperwork.

Your accountant will use these records to create a profit and loss account for you, which will let you know how much income was generated and what expenses were paid out over the financial year, and whether you had made a profit or a loss. The more detailed records you keep, the easier it will be to answer any questions that your accountant or the Inland Revenue may have regarding your tax return.

Your business accounts need to be stored safely for five years after the normal filing deadline of 31st January and this will also include the safe storage of your appointment books and business diaries.

This business guide has been written for the UK market – please seek professional advice for other Countries on Legal Requirements.

~~~~~~

CHAPTER 7

How To Write A Business Plan

Your Road Map to Success

Your self-employed business life is going to be very hectic and even more so if you also have the commitment of another job, or are bringing up a family. There will be telephone calls to make, letters to write, advertising to plan and client databases to build – let alone the day-to-day emergencies, which will pop up quite frequently sapping your valuable time. It's all going to take a lot of hard work and total dedication.

Short-term issues should not divert you from your long-term goals and crucial business planning. Writing a business plan is not as daunting as you may first think, you are merely encapsulating your objectives and writing them down such as what you intend to achieve and what resources you'll need. Think of it a bit like going on a long journey from say Southampton to Manchester. What do you intend to achieve from the journey (to get from Southampton to Manchester) and what resources will you need to accomplish that (a car, some sort of road map, fuel, road tax and a drink and packet of sandwiches maybe).

So what type of plans are needed? Well basically there are three.

1. An Objective Master Plan
2. A Cash Flow Plan.
3. A Business Finance Plan

Let's take a look at each one individually.

The Objective Master Plan

Do you actually know where you're going in your hair or beauty business today, next month or even next year? Is that information logged somewhere? Do you have a written master plan for your future success or do you just have hopes and dreams floating around in your head? A lot of self-employed people just hope for the best without giving a second thought to a plan of action for creating the type of business they'd be happy with. They've become conditioned into having a wishbone rather than a backbone, as that good old saying goes. Unfortunately, a very big mistake.

There are so many supporting reasons for writing an objective master plan as you embark on your future, which is an important aspect in the creation of a successful business. Without one in place that lists exactly what you hope to achieve and accomplish, it's highly unlikely that you'll succeed let alone reach your desired fortune if it's all just pie in the sky.

Your objective plan will be filled with all your exciting hopes, ideas and aspirations for your growing business and it will always serve as inspiration to you. There is nothing quite like writing down your forecasts on paper and over the coming years watching them happen. Your objective master plan should also include other personal aspects of your life as well and not only be written about your business ones. Embrace these other areas and include things such as family, relationships, holidays, material things and anything else you should desire. It will be all about putting the pieces together making them fit into your work and life puzzle, allowing them to harmonise together. Think of your plan as an aspiration for the life that you want and then create it over a three-year time-span (long-term goals), broken down into twelve monthly segments (short-term goals).

One point to remember here is that in business there is never a straight path that can be followed. We tend to get from A to B and then from B to C in a sort of wiggly wobbly fashion – known as diversion. Slight diversification off the straight and narrow is totally acceptable as long as you are always focused on the end result, whether that's a short-term goal or a long-term goal, and get yourself back on track.

Even though you will be setting a forward thinking plan, it's not set in stone as things will happen beyond your control, your desires and priorities will change and your experience will grow. The important point is to write your plan for the future in today's context as if you had already achieved the goals that are listed, given your current abilities. Your plan will become a source of stimulation to you over the coming months as you read and re-read them.

To write in today's context you'd put something like: "During this year I will double my client list and I will put one new marketing activity in place each and every week. I'll have a website up and running by the fourth month and I will have designed a new brochure by month five. In month seven my Facebook business page will be up and running and will be getting twenty new Likes each week. My family and I will take a two-week holiday in the spring and a short weekend break in the autumn".

An easy trap to fall into is that of starting out in business, fulfilling a couple of steps on your objective master plan and then running out of time and motivation. If you're hesitant about guiding your business through efficiently to its profitability stage, then you may be better off not even writing a plan!

Anyone can go into business expecting to earn a fortune, but if they don't have plans, actions and goals outlining their road-map to success – how on earth are they going to get there and reach their desired destiny. By putting pen to paper and actually writing your plans down will help you to understand what it is that you want to achieve over a certain time-span from your business and will allow you to put in motion the activities that will help you to get there. It really is as easy as that. Your objective master plan will be your road-map to success for without one, you won't get very far.

Once your objective master plan has been written it shouldn't be stuffed away in a draw somewhere out of sight. It should be close to hand and used as an inspiration tool – or you could say a kick up the butt! By checking your plan on a monthly basis will keep you on the right track and you'll be able to clarify whether your business growth is indeed progressing at the right pace. Your vision must be one that will literally pull you into the future, will scare you a little bit and make your heart beat a little faster than normal whenever you read it. Make you aspirations very specific, measurable, and realistic and at the same time a bit of a stretch.

The Cash Flow Plan

When you plan a day of retail therapy you generally write yourself a shopping list, or you may just store it in your mind. This list could include new jeans, jumper, shoes, a CD, and some luxury smellies for the bathroom. You stuff a £20 note into your purse and off you go on your journey. Come the end of the day you are going to be left feeling really despondent and unenthused, as your twenty pounds didn't stretch as far as you hoped it would. You just didn't have enough cash to buy everything you needed and wanted that was on your list!

A cash flow plan is no different and is very much tied into your objective master plan. You know what you want, but have you got the available funds to get it? You need to be able to forecast the flow of cash that you have available – thus a cash flow plan.

You can write your cash flow forecast on a month by month scale:

- Plan a forecast of the money you anticipate coming into your business - services rendered, invoices rendered, products sold, miscellaneous income, and any capital you may invest. Simply put it means making a list of all the money you expect to earn on a realistic scale and try not to over-exaggerate here. This is the cash flow coming in.

- Plan a forecast of the money you will need to pay out to suppliers for purchases, wages to yourself (drawings), any tax due, marketing and advertising costs, telephone bill, fuel costs, professional fees, general expenses, bank charges, insurance and any other expenses.

It's very important to make realistic assumptions here and to try and account for every eventuality, which is sometimes easier said than done!

By keeping your cash flow forecast in line with your bank account will help to throw up any situations when your need for cash is at its greatest. For example in the leaner months when you may find that business is slower than usual, you'll be able to plan your cash accordingly to meet pending payments and expenses. Those lean months that will flag up from time to time may not be the time to invest in training, or to expand into a new product range or to kit yourself out with a new uniform. Don't forget that most businesses fit into the feast and famine category and over time you'll get to know when yours will be.

Once you have your objective and cash flow plans written you'll be able to work out your personal survival budget and what you would like to earn from your business. An easy way to do this is to calculate your turnover from the past three months (this is the money you received for services rendered) and then take away all your expenses, excluding personal drawings. This amount can now be divided between three months and this will give you your average monthly income, and then divide by four will give you your average weekly income. From this income figure you would then work out what you would like to earn, or can afford to earn on a weekly basis. If there is any money left in the pot after all the expenses have been paid and accounted for, is your business profit.

By doing this exercise regularly over three months, six months and a year will enable you to understand the viability of your business.

You will then be able to ask yourself the following questions:

- Is there sufficient turnover in my business?
- Am I earning enough in wages to meet my needs?
- Do I need to look at my pricing structures and improve them to increase my turnover?
- Do I need to add a new service or product to generate extra income?

Taking time to track the progress of your turnover will throw some light onto how your business is moving forward and growing. Ideally you need to see a situation whereby each quarter the business has improved on the last quarter, even if it's only a slight difference, and then by checking it on a year to year basis. By the time you have been in business for a couple of years you will be prepared for those impending lean months that you know will be looming (we all have them) so that you can plan your cash flow accordingly and also look forward with anticipation to those forthcoming fruitful months – the famine and the feast.

The Business Finance Plan

This is a more thorough and comprehensive plan than the two above, and its intended use is for financial backing from a bank or investor.

This plan combines your objective master plan and your cash flow plan but on a 'no fail' basis. It must be thorough and conservative regarding the future of the business along with projected sales and costs, especially if you are handing it over to a bank manager or a financial investor.

If you do need financial backing for the future and growth of your business, your financial backer will need instilled confidence in you and your judgement. However, your business finance plan must achieve a balance between optimism and realism in order to persuade those that you are seeking either a bank loan or a business investment.

So what will you need to put into your business finance plan? Here are a few necessary elements:

- What is the business – this will be a brief overview including when it was started, what is its nature, what has been its previous trading history.
- The management structure – who you are and what's your previous employment and qualification history, what are your strengths and weaknesses in management, and how you will recruit if additional staff are required.
- The service and/or product – a simple description of what you offer and your pricing structure and how it will be developed over time to meet current trends.
- Who is your client – who is your target market that your service and/or product is aimed at, how often do they buy.
- How will you market your business – compile a list of all your proposed marketing strategies?

- Who is your competition – their size and position in the marketplace, what are their strengths and what are their weaknesses.
- What is the potential for business growth – over a five-year time span?
- How much investment or loan is required from the bank or lender – and how you will pay it back, and what is your exit strategy if the business fails.
- A full financial analysis of the forecasted profits for the next three-years.

As you can see from above the business finance plan is quite heavy going and is not something that can be put together on a tea-break. This plan will need thorough research and will need to be presented in a professional manner prior to submitting to any finance lender.

Your objective, cash flow and finance business plan shouldn't be written and then forgotten about. They should be used as a reference and progression tool for your business. By returning to them on a regular basis will enable you to make changes for the better, it will highlight any areas that you may feel need your immediate attention to avoid a spiralling downturn, and will provide enthusiasm and inspiration to push your business onto its next level of growth.

Once you get going you'll build up a momentum with your business planning and things should go from good to great. By making sure that you have the above strategies in place from the onset will all help to make your business run as a smooth operation. Remember the saying – 'If you fail to plan you'll plan to fail'.

~~~~~~

CHAPTER 8

Putting Yourself Out There

Your Gateway to Marketing

So your beauty business is all set up and raring to go, or maybe you have been at it for some time now, and one of your biggest worries is how to get more clients – a usual dilemma! If you just sit around waiting for the next appointment to come your way you might have to wait some time unless you become proactive and get amongst it.

If you're new to business and need to build up your client list, the best place to start is with your family, friends and neighbours. Let's look at each of those on an individual basis.

Family – No doubt you used family members as you went through your training process, as this is quite usual.

The family members that you have been practicing on now need to be aware that you're building a business that has little or no reputation and that if they want to see you succeed they should be willing to write good-standing testimonials for you about the services that you have provided to them. You will be able to use these testimonials to promote yourself. Family members can also be involved in helping to distribute your promotional material to *their* friends that are unknown to you. A good reputation will spread like wild-fire and at this point in time your family will be able to help spread the word to others for you.

Friends – The same approach as above will apply for friends now that you're up and running as a business owner. Certain systems will need to be put in place as this is how you will be earning some income, whether on a part-time basis in the beginning or as a single source of income later on.

You will need to make a decision here about your pricing strategy as a lot of friends will probably be eager to use your beauty service but will they expect something for nothing! To help, you could just ask for a donation of payment against the product that you use or as a gesture for the time spent. You may also be able to do 'tit-for-tat' meaning that they may have a service or something to offer you in exchange for your expertise. Don't fall into the trap here of letting the majority of your friends persuade you to do their nails or haircut for free, you have to draw the line somewhere. After all you're running a business aren't you and friends and acquaintances should respect this.

In the same instance you will be able to build on your testimonials here and ask each friend for referrals from their family members and any unknown friends and work colleagues that they may have.

Neighbours (direct) – These are people that you see on a regular basis as they are the ones that live in your street.

Make a scheduled time whereby you can go along to their home to put them in the picture about your new business venture. Give them as much information as possible on the beauty service that you provide that you feel would be of interest to them, and leave them with one of your brochures/leaflets. Let them know that you offer a reward system and that they will get a 'special gift' if they refer you to one of their friends or family members who makes an appointment with you, and this will be an incentive for them to promote you to whoever they can.

Neighbours (indirect) – These are the people that live in your immediate surroundings, perhaps taking in a handful of roads close by.

Now I'm a great believer that home delivered mail-shots are an absolute waste of time as you can never be sure if you are targeting your market or not because you are unaware of the occupants and their lifestyle that live there. But in the case of promoting your new business venture and the fact that you are also a resident of the immediate area will be well worth the shoe-leather, and you could even go so far as offering them a complimentary discount for being a neighbour of yours.

Building Your First Client List

To get your client list built, you need to think of the many other people that you know who your acquaintances are. These people are everywhere and can include your work colleagues (former or current), your spouse's work colleagues, the people who run the corner shop, your dentist or doctor, the guys at the vets, the swimming pool and the gym. If you're a parent then your target list should also include the mums and dads at the school gates and at your child's activity clubs.

Take an hour or so to sit down and brainstorm a list of everybody, yes everybody that you know regardless of whether it's just those that you encounter on a daily basis or those that you just see once in a while. You'll be quite surprised at how long your list will be – and any number of these people could have great potential to become one of your clients in the future! After your list is compiled, your next step will be to organise some sort of time-plan for seeking those people out. Put this process into effect with everyone on your list so that you make a point of actually 'bumping' into them because you know where they will be at a certain time of day – and voilà with leaflet in hand – another potential client has been targeted. Never leave home without a handful of leaflets or business cards ..... just in case!

Joining your local networking group is also a great way to get to know people in your area. If it's a business networking group this will provide you with an opportunity to interact with like minded business owners that will be able to assist you and give you support.

So there's a couple of ways to build your customer list from the very beginning, and with this process of targeting those known to you, you will gradually see the momentum build, which can in fact happen quite quickly.

Maybe you already have valuable client information such as addresses, phone numbers and email addresses stored away somewhere. Well now's the time to start building a database so that information is easily retrievable as and when you need it. You can feed this information into spreadsheets, mail-merges, Word document table formats or even hand-written record cards. By keeping an organised system going right from the very beginning will give you the necessary tools to be able to contact your clients at a moment's notice without having to traipse through appointment books and the like.

~~~~~~

CHAPTER 9

Your Target Market

Is Anyone There?

When choosing your service to provide, or product to sell, it's important to be sure that there is a market for it and that it is something that customers and clients will want to buy from you. You need to find out what people are spending their money on in the hair and beauty industry and do what it takes to maximise on it. These people will then become your Target Market.

You need to appeal to a perceptive sector of the market as you cannot possibly sell to everyone and there will only be a proportion of people interested in what you're offering. Don't make the mistake of trying to market to everybody. Look for gaps and opportunities in the market place and exploit them if you can and this means spotting trends as they happen.

By having a basic understanding of who your client is will help you with your marketing plan, and by having an array of information on them will make it easier to sell to them. What they all have in common will allow you to target new clients more easily and you can then direct your marketing into that specific category, rather than going in blind and mailing to the masses or placing adverts in totally irrelevant publications. Right from the very beginning, if you don't know who your target market is you're setting yourself up for failure. By knowing who they are will help you to sharpen up your marketing and you'll be able to communicate it more effectively to that specific group of people.

So who is your ideal client? Who is your business for? What is their general profile? What do they all have in common? Think about it now. Find out about the type of client you want to sell to and push your marketing in their direction.

To find out about your client profile and their common traits, which is also known as a niche, you'll need to do some sort of survey, which is always easier to do on *existing* clients if you already have them, than on those who are your potential clients. Once you have researched who your niche is and what their similar characteristics and requirements are, will allow you to tailor your services to meet their particular needs, as you will find that these common traits will lead to similar buying decisions from other like-minded individuals.

So Who is Your Target Market?

You can understand who your target market is by doing some research on them. A great way to capture this information is just through general conversation with your existing clients and after the appointment with them making notes of your findings. This will be a great help towards your marketing efforts as you'll be better informed where to focus your efforts and attention on.

Below is a generalised list of all the different types of research information that you can collect on your target market to better understand them.

- Home – What type of house do they live in? Is it on an estate, or in a village, is it in the city, or maybe a remote dwelling in the country? How many bedrooms, bathrooms and reception rooms does it have?
- Area – Are you able to locate your target market easily? Where do they live, and in what type of area? How far are you willing to travel to get to them to provide your service if your mobile?
- Marital Status – What is their circumstance with regards to their relationships? Are they single, in a partnership, married or divorced?

- Family - How many children do they have, how many girls and how many boys, and what are their ages? Are they school age children or in further education. In what environment did they gain their education, independent or mainstream?
- Class - Is their social standing important? Are they from the lower to middle class bracket or are they the high class and affluent type where money is no object and they don't buy on price alone?
- Car - What type of car do they drive? Is it from an inexpensive range which could pre-dispose them to just making do, or do they drive a prestige car and expect all the quality and luxuries that they have come to know and expect?
- Groceries – Do they buy their groceries from a large National multi-chain supermarket or do they frequently use the small independent shop for their weekly goods, which will also include personal service?
- Clothes - Where do they shop for their clothes? Can they usually be seen as a patron to designer shops in affluent locations, or the mainstream stores in shopping centres, or is their usual shopping spree done on the Internet?
- Tabloids - What newspapers do they read and is this on a daily or weekly basis. What are their favourite consumer magazines or trade

publications, and what triggers them to purchase that particular publication?

- Self Esteem - Will your service touch on a psychological factor for them? Could your service appeal to those wishing to be seen to always have the best of everything?
- Lifestyle – Will your service relate to a certain type of lifestyle? Does your target market like to 'keep up with the Joneses' or do they like to set a new trend in motion being the first to try something new and fashionable?
- Price - Are they price conscious and only buy on price alone, always looking for the cheapest option, or do they understand that price can be a reflection of the quality of service that is provided and value for money?
- Frequency - Will they use your service on a regular and consistent basis and become a long-standing loyal client which is most certainly the type you want, or will they be here today and gone tomorrow with a one-off isolated appointment?
- Networking - Do they belong to any groups, clubs or alliances that you can also join in order to get close to them? Can you get to know them by visiting and participating in certain types of forums and clubs?
- Social Media - Do they frequently visit social media sites, if so, which ones and how often? How

many followers and friends do they have on there which could also potentially be your target market?

So who is your ideal client? What's their profile? What are their common traits? Are you able to do a survey to find out?

Compiling the above information will take a considerable amount of time and effort, and once in receipt of that information you will need to place it into a database of some sort so that it can be added to as new people become clients and reviewed on a regular basis. An Excel document is always a good place for storage of such details as is a table format in a Word processor. Failing that a simple hand-drafted document would suffice. Once you have a clear picture of whom your potential client is, it is quite possible to purchase a list of people in your area with the same matching qualities as your target, should you wish to pursue that route.

When working in clients homes keep an eye out for items that could build their profile. Things like newspapers, magazines and used shopping bags. Also make a mental note of the type of car they drive and the classification of the area in which they live. All these things will help you to understand their profile better.

By undertaking a thorough market research will enable you to target your client more effectively with regards to your advertising both online and offline, it will provide you with priorities regarding your networking activities, and will assist in the design of your sales and promotional literature. For example, the quality of your brochure – does it need to be a super high-class glossy one or will a standardised cheaper version do. If you're providing your service for a lot of wealthy clients you most certainly don't want hand-made computer based leaflets to hand out to them. Instead go for nice glossy printed ones that have been professionally designed and printed. There are many ways that you can get your message across, however you must ensure that you go about it in a cost-effective way. Spending your hard-earned cash on marketing activities should be measured and calculated so that you don't fall into the trap of over-spending on say an advertising campaign that has little or no response from your target market by advertising in completely the wrong type of publication. The overall cost of your communication should be checked and calculated against how much income was generated from responses and how much profit went into the bank.

If you happen to be at the start-up stage in your beauty business whereby you don't have any clients and are therefore unable to work out their common profile you can research your target market by talking and listening to other allied industries. Make an acquaintance with other beauty therapists, hair stylists, make-up artists and nail technicians in your area and this way you will be able to glean the information needed in order to build your client profile. You'll find that most small business owners love to talk about themselves and about how their business is doing (or not doing!). This will give you valuable information that you can use to identify your potential client.

You will no doubt be in competition with other established businesses in your area, and the mere fact that this competition exists should not worry or deter you. Competition is healthy, as they say, and it means that there is a ready and willing audience for you to market to, you just need to be able to offer your clients some sort of extra value to your service provision.

Eventually you'll find the type of client that you actually love to be of service to, you know the type .... plenty of repeat appointments, money no object, always completely satisfied, etc. Well the way to get more of the type of client who you consider to be a perfect match is to look at where this client came from, how they found out about you. Perhaps it was through a referral, maybe from a leaflet you placed at a certain establishment or maybe from an advert you placed in a particular magazine. By knowing how your client come to be will help you in leaps and bounds to attract the same or similar sort. Create a spreadsheet to record where your clients come from and review it often. Find out what marketing element is working for you and what's not, and do more of the stuff that's bringing in your ideal target market.

~~~~~

CHAPTER 10

How Are You Selling Yourself?

Are You Promoting The Benefits?

The message that you need to get across should be all about letting your client know about the benefits that your service or product will mean to them.

The 'benefits' of your business are how you make your client feel, what it does to their self-esteem and the value that you are going to add for them. These are the benefits that need to be enforced into every paragraph of your advertising and your promotional material helping you to clearly stand out from the rest. The words that you write need to be all about what your client needs and wants, well at least what you think they need and want. The words you write should not be all about you and what you've got. They are not interested in those features. What they do want to know about is how your service is going to benefit them, what experience it will bring and what you can actually do for them. You need to think about how you're going to massively improve their life when they do business with you.

Your prospective client isn't interested in how brilliant you are, whether you are by far the best in town, how long you've been established, or what qualifications you hold. They're just not interested. They don't want to read all about you, you, you and your huge ego trip. These are your 'features' and quite bluntly no one really cares about them. Features are boring, uninteresting, and don't have enough information attached to them that will compel the prospective client into making an informed decision about contacting you or not!

The features of your business which won't impress your client are:

- Your length of time in the industry
- The brand of product you use
- Your low or high prices
- Your smart and impressive website
- Who your previous clients are
- The qualifications and experience you have
- The location of your business and it's great car parking facilities
- Your sign-written car/van that you drive

These are all features (and good ones I might add) of your business. Features should still be used however, but not as the main context of your sales material. People don't buy features, they don't care about your industry experience as it makes no odds to them – all they care about is the quality of the service that you will be providing to them and the experience that it will bring.

Focus on the positive results of your service. People buy results. What is it that you're going to bring to them, what is the benefit of using you, what is the experience that they will have? Focus on your advantages. What problems do you solve? If you surf through the Internet you will probably see that most beauty therapist, hair stylists, make-up artists and nail technicians are all hammering home their features, me, me, me, me!

You'll find that typical paper-based advertising the sort that you see in newspapers and community magazines from an extensive array of businesses usually go along the lines of: their logo, followed by a feature, followed by bullet points with more of their features, followed with their telephone number and address. Where are the benefits to the client?

Try this out for a little exercise. Go and get a local magazine, Yellow Pages or newspaper and thumb through the pages looking at all the adverts placed there. What do you see? Plenty of features I expect. I took a look through our community magazine that dropped on the doormat this month and it was filled with things like:

- Painter & Decorator – All Interior Work Undertaken.

- Cleaning Services – Domestic Cleaning and Office Cleaning.
- Building Services – Free Estimates and Advice. No Obligation.
- Bouncy Castle Hire – Established in 2004.
- School of Motoring – Fully Qualified Instructor.
- Pet Surgery – Friendly Family Run Business.
- Hair Salon – Professional Cutting and Colouring Specialists.
- Beauty Salon – listing every conceivable qualification.

And the list could go on and on. Boring, uninteresting and not compelling enough for the client to pick up the phone because it's not saying what's in it for them, they're only listing features, me, me, me, me, me. Those were the main taglines for those companies. What value do they offer their customer or client? None whatsoever. Not one of them is selling the benefit, the end result. Instead they are all selling themselves and their ego.

They want to know how you're going to make a difference, they want to know what value you are going to give to them and what problem or need of theirs you are going to solve for them.

Remember benefits first – features later.

Getting The Message Across

The benefit of any hair and beauty service is how it's going to make your client look and feel. It's the emotional experience that is attached to the service which is the benefit, and it's that which must be promoted in order to sell it. That's what the client is buying – the end result and not the name of the service provided such as manicure, facial or leg wax.

Stating the benefits of your service is what you should be concentrating on when writing the copy for your adverts, the copy for your sales literature, your website and your business cards. In fact anywhere and everywhere that your client sees your written words should have the emphasis focused on the benefits to them.

Here are a few pointers in the right direction of what a benefit is and how you could include them in your advertising and marketing:

- How is your service going to make your customer feel – a benefit
- How is your service going to make your customer look – a benefit

- What need of theirs will you be fulfilling – a benefit
- What is it going to do to their self-esteem – a benefit
- What added value are you going to bring – a benefit
- What is the final result that you are selling –a benefit
- What incentive to book now are you offering – a benefit

You need to stop thinking features, or how brilliant you are, or how good your service or product is, as the client will judge that for themselves. Instead start to fixate on your clients mind and about the benefits that you will bring to them through experiencing your service or product. Sell the emotion, the outcome, the final result of your service, and sell how it will make them feel by booking an appointment with you.

Put this into practice when you next place an advert, or design a brand new leaflet or are writing copy for your website. What does your message say to your potential client? Your advert must sell the benefits of the end result and not just the features of your service.

Selling The End Result

So how do you sell the end result? You need to take a step back and think about what your service provides as an end result and what problem does it solve? Your client is buying the end result so the final outcome of your service is what you should sell. Make sure that all your literature reflects the end result – the benefits.

Let's take some general everyday scenarios here:

- When you book an appointment at a hair salon you don't see the trendy surroundings, the immaculate staff uniform and the adequate parking facilities. Features. What you imagine is your beautiful shining and conditioned hair, a fantastic cut that is the best you've ever had and how you will feel knowing you look absolutely fabulous. You see the end result and the pleasure that it will bring. The benefit.

- When you book a mobile nail technician you don't see her expensive kit box or marvel at her state-of-the-art UV curing lamp. Features. What you do see is your stumpy short nails and ragged cuticles transformed into perfectly enhanced extensions with stunning polish or nail art. You see the end result – the benefit.

- When you buy a joint of meat you don't just see the meat in its plastic wrapper. Instead you imagine the roast dinner with delicious potatoes and vegetables and perhaps you even see the table setting in your mind's eye. So gone is the vision of a piece of cold meat sitting tightly on a polystyrene tray wrapped in film, and in its place you can see a lovely dining experience, perhaps with friends. The benefit.

- When your front lawn is in dire need of attention, you don't care what special chemicals will be used, you don't care how long the gardener has been in business and you certainly don't care what van he'll be driving. What you imagine is a beautiful lush lawn that is short, well trimmed and very green. You might even see the look of envy on your neighbour's faces! The benefit.

Are you getting the picture here? In everywhere that you are using words, whether written or spoken, it is a skill to master the ability to write or speak good copy that sells. People think in pictures so provide an image to be placed in your clients mind. I expect that images came to mind for you when you read all the above scenarios didn't they? How well do you think you are scoring with your copy writing? Is your client seeing the picture? Are you selling the end result or purely the name of your service? If it's the latter you need to stop selling the word such as an Aromatherapy Massage and start selling the end result, start selling the emotion, start solving the clients problem and start selling the value that it will bring.

Now, go through your own adverts and literature (leaflets, etc) and take a long hard and critical look at your copy writing. Have you written just a long list of bullet points such as Eyebrow Shaping, Cut and Blow-Dry or Special Occasion Make-up. What benefits to the client are you promoting? Be honest with yourself – is there room for improvement? If so, start now. Start writing effective copy that tempts your them into doing business with you!

~~~~~

CHAPTER 11

Setting Your Prices

Are You Being Paid What You Deserve?

What if you realised that everything you thought you knew about setting your prices was wrong. Setting prices for your service is such a challenging task and for many small business owners the big question is how do you get it just right? How do you come up with the best price that the client will be happy to pay, with the best profit margins for your hair or beauty venture?

Your pricing structure is extremely important as you really need to get it right from the onset. If you charge an unbelievably high price for your services you will price yourself out of the market, and if you drastically undercut and price way too cheaply you'll become a threat to your competitors and run the risk of bad feelings between you and them. Do your market research thoroughly at this stage and gain as much information about your competitors pricing structures as possible and try to keep the consistency of similar prices going. You will need to take into consideration however their quality of service, their reputation in the industry, their longevity of practice and their comparable qualities to you and your business.

There are a couple of pricing strategies that I would like to share with you, but first I must make it clear that what is right for one face business may not necessarily be the best for another due to many influential circumstances such as location, experience and nerve!

Have a look at the three different pricing strategies below and see which one your business fits into:

1. **Do you feel compelled to put your price in line with your competitor?**

    Are you setting your prices to match the competitors in your area? Is this the right thing for you to do? Is this the best market price for the best value? Where did they get their pricing strategy from anyway? Did they just pluck this figure from thin air? Is their service superior or inferior to yours? Do you have the same skill-set and are they faster or slower in their service than you? Does their business have the same over-heads and advertising expenses? Do they have staff to pay, or a commercial car or van to run? Are they working the business as a part-time pocket money hobby or as a full-time business? And finally – why do you compare yourself to your competitor?

2. **Do you feel that you should lower your price to get more business?**

Maybe to win more business you have decided to lower your prices to beat your competition. Lowering your prices is by far the worst thing you can do, if you do that then you are in fact 'buying your work'. This is going to do nothing for the way your client perceives you as you will very fast become known as cheap, poor quality, and amateurish. You're also making it hard for everyone else by de-valuing the industry as a whole. You'll eventually be in a situation where you'll find it almost impossible to increase your prices overtime as a precedent would have been set by you. Is that what you have gone into business for, to offer your skill and services for a cheap price? If the client wants a budget price then she can go seek an alternative source. Even in this economic downturn, lowering your prices will be the worst thing you can possibly do.

3. **Do you charge over and above the normal rate?**

Are you brave enough to charge over and above the industry norm? Are you a first-class therapist, stylist, artist or technician with an elite skill? Great, then charge for it. Don't devalue yourself; ask for what you deserve to be paid and be recognized for the value that you are adding to your clients lives.

It's a big mistake to believe that you can't increase your prices, especially in a bad economic climate. A total myth. Don't under-sell yourself. A word of warning here though – you'll be run out of town if you charge high fees for just a bog-standard service. You must be exceptional in what you do, willing to go the extra mile by adding immense value to the lives of your clients, then indeed you can charge the high fees you so rightly deserve!

So looking back at the three different pricing strategies, which one do you fall into within your business? Are you content with where you are now?

Clients Buy Experiences

As competition in our industry has grown immensely I often hear about make-up artists, not necessarily in my area, charging ridiculously low prices just to get themselves out there. Those who charge very, very low fees really need to wake up and smell the coffee and divide the income between the labour time involved, the getting ready time involved, the getting to the appointment time involved (if mobile), the cleaning of the kit when getting home time involved, let alone the fuel, the insurance, the administration costs, etc, etc, etc. De-valuation and poor price indications will have a moral knock-on effect.

You may feel like you're in a catch-22 situation when you first start up in the industry as you realise that you've got a long way to go with regards to skill and speed. You'll probably feel the urge to charge a fairly low price in the beginning just to get yourself known as you may not feel confident in charging what other businesses are. Big mistake unless you don't have any intentions of running this new enterprise of yours as a business, and are just going down the hobby route! When you calculate all the costs involved which includes preparation, fuel (45p per mile at the moment) and travel time, your labour charge for when you are providing your service and your product costs, all these things will add up. Most often a one-hour appointment will actually take three hours of your time as it's all of the logistics combined. If you divide a low-fee that you may be charging by the three hours, at the end of the day is it actually worth it? Stacking shelves in a supermarket would be financially better and you wouldn't have the stress-factor of running a business to contend with either!

There are, however, clients out there who will only buy on price alone and not on quality and you'll find that 'budget' is their middle name. Maybe you know someone like that, always looking for a cheap bargain or a massive discount, or maybe complaining about a service in order to get the price down! However, it's also worth remembering that there are people out there who will always pay that little bit extra for value, for the experience it brings, and for the self-esteem it bestows. They will buy the perceived value. These clients can afford it; in fact 5-10% of your existing clients can afford it – so go the extra mile and add-on an extra element, maybe an up-sell to your service that is different to what you sell to the majority. You will always have those who are willing to pay for an elite version of what you do at a far higher price.

As you can see from the list below there will always be people who will pay extra for value, experience and for their own self-esteem, which includes:

- Those who travel first-class – it's the same train or plane that transports the people to their destination and it gets them all there at the same time, but there will always be those who will pay to be more comfortable, and to feel more valued than the rest and for a better experience.
- There will always be those who dress themselves and their family in designer clothes and wouldn't dream of anything less.
- There will always be those who patron the most expensive and lavish restaurants and wouldn't be seen in a fast-food outlet.

- Those who will pay extra to enhance their image, their self-esteem and that of their children's and their home by being the first to choose something that is the best, is new, different, unique and unusual - keeping up with the Joneses' so to speak.

Think about your buying behaviour as well. What do you pay extra for to provide you with extra value for money? Do you firstly decide what you want to buy and then go and look for it, or do you decide on the price to spend and then go looking for the item to fit the cost (this is buying on price alone and taking nothing else into consideration). Make a list of your 'price no option' purchases. Shoes and handbags might be one of yours – it certainly isn't one of mine!

Incidentally, I must also point out that no-one should ever have the right to haggle about your prices as they are instantly de-valuing you and your skill that you've worked hard to achieve. If someone asks you for a discount, say 10%, you could try the answer "Yeah sure. So what 10% shall I take off my service for you – maybe I'll miss off applying the top coat to your painted nails then shall I? It gives you the upper hand and works every time. It's a fabulous remark, and my husband even uses it in his double-glazing business - "Yeah sure I can cut the costs, he says, so which window shall I leave the glass out of?"!!!

Let's recap - never think about lowering your prices, instead think about how you can get more by adding extra value to your service that you are providing. Add on a bonus product or service to what you already offer giving your client an incentive to book an appointment with you. So go on, give it a try – add something of better value to what you already do, and then aggressively market it to your clients. You'll find that there will be willing purchasers of your elite/bespoke service and you wouldn't want to miss out on that 5-10% of those who are willing to pay more for a superior version of what you already do, would you?

~~~~~

CHAPTER 12

Client Needs

What Does Your Client Really Want?

Once you understand your client profile and just who your target market is, the next stage is to market your service or product to them in such a way that what you offer is so irresistible to them that they just can't refuse it.

To do this effectively you will need to become perceptive to your clients needs, wants and desires. Needs, wants and desires are at the forefront of all business sales. If your client doesn't want it, doesn't need it or doesn't desire it – then they simply will not buy it. It's as easy as that!

Let's take a closer look at needs, wants and desires:

- A Need – is a requirement or necessity of something in need or something that requires a course of action, as in help.
- A Want – can be a wish for something, or something to be attended to in a specified way.
- A Desire – is a request for an unsatisfied longing or craving, as in a heart's desire for something.

Some examples of your clients needs, wants and desires could be:

- The client *needs* to have her roots done.
- The client *wants* to have a new hair style.
- The client *desires* to have hair extensions.

We usually find that needs and wants arise from a problematic situation. In other words, your client has a problem that she would like you to solve. By looking for the problems that your clients are experiencing will enable you to understand their needs, wants and desires and this in turn will be the key to targeting your market with a service or product that becomes an enticing offer.

In order to sell a product or service to a customer or client is all about getting inside their heads and really understanding what makes them tick. What problem can you solve for them by providing your hair or beauty service? What needs will they have when you are actually providing the treatment? What desire of theirs will you be able to fulfil prior to the appointment, during the appointment and after the service has taken place? Your client will be looking for reassurance of quality and professionalism from someone else who can take control of their needs, wants and desires.

People don't just buy for the sake of it. There is always an underlying problem to be solved, or a need or a want or a desire to be realised. Take these additional points as an example:

- People purchase a car because they don't want to walk
- People book a window cleaner because they don't want to clean their own windows
- People go on holiday because they deserve a well-earned break
- People buy expensive shoes because they desire to look well groomed
- People buy a new coat because the winter is coming and they need to be warm
- People buy anti-ageing skin care because they want their wrinkles to disappear
- People buy food and water because they want to live
  . . . and the list could go on and on and on!

Every service or product that is purchased is generally done so to fulfil needs, wants, desires and problems.

Go one step further and think about all the services that you have used over the past month and write them down. Now attach a need, a want, a desire or a problem to them all. Do the same for your monthly purchases, everything you spent your hard-earned cash on even if you only bought it on a whim (at the time you must have thought you had a need for it)! It's a great little exercise to do because it really does highlight the necessity on how you can attract your clients by identifying what it is they actually want from you

Are You Interested In Your Client?

Start becoming genuinely interested in other people and what they have to say, either to you or to other people. In other words, become a professional eavesdropper! Listen out for needs, wants and desires and act on them as soon as you can. Is there something that you can offer them, can you help in anyway. Think of an angle - make a habit of listening in to others people's conversations and make a mental note of their unfulfilled needs that they talk of and work on a way that you can use it to your marketing advantage. There are certain words that you need to listen out for. As soon as you hear the sentence starters listed below, you need to adjust your concentration level and prick-up your radar.

How often have you heard people say:
"If only I could....... "I wish I ....
"I'd love to ...."You just can't get ....
"There's nowhere that sells..........

These are golden opportunities just waiting to be acted upon. What needs, wants and desires are presenting themselves to you? How can you build on your client relationship by adding value for them? Positive words are also good to be on the lookout for as well, because if another business person is being praised and recommended by others for their service, you too need to be doing whatever it is that they're doing, and do it just as well or even better. Be on the ready to listen out for any negative statements as well that your clients may speak about such as "the salon I went into last week never did this..." or "the hair-dresser was supposed to do that..." These words are signs of dissatisfaction from previous experiences – can you act on them and fill a gap in the market? How could you have made it better for them? If you're hearing the same problem time and time again there could be an unmet need out there. Maybe their needs are blocked in some way? Are there opportunities where your products or services can make a different impact into the market? Have new needs been created by changes going on around you, i.e., social, economical, cultural or technological. Can you capitalize on anything here?

Do whatever you can to make your clients life easier by paying special attention to their needs, wants and desires and not just your achievement. Add some extra happiness, give them an amazing experience from just using your company, and by making them feel special you'll be surprised at how they'll view you and your business as you will certainly stand out from the rest. By having needs, wants and desires catered for that in turn will lead to more people seeking out your service. So listen out, and act as soon as you can. Is there something that you can offer, can you help them in any way possible?

~~~~~~

CHAPTER 13

Client Care

Just How Good Is Your Client Care?

Running your hair or beauty business is not all about providing your service just for the fee being paid to you. How the client perceives you and the support of the additional care that you provide will go a long way in building your image and your business model. It's all about going the extra mile and doing just a little bit more for each and every one of your existing clients and potential clients by providing a first-class service with additional unexpected things that they didn't expect that will put you way ahead of the competition.

Good client care stems from how in-sync you are with the people who do business with you and those who use your service. Good client care means that you are genuinely interested in serving them to your best ability and are always on the lookout on how you can make improvements.

Your number one priority in business is client satisfaction. That's a priority. Unfortunately a lot of people in business view their customer or client as an interruption to work. I'm sure your know the sort of person I mean – they're the ones who tut-tut when you go into their shop and ask for advice right in the middle of when they're doing an important job like stacking the shelves or those who sigh loudly because you've interrupted them changing a light-bulb!! For goodness sake – without the customer or client who makes the business go round there wouldn't be a business to go round or the immortal light-bulb to change. Pause here for a moment and think about a recent time when you encountered appalling customer service from someone. How did that make you feel?

Another priority is how you handle client enquiries, a big area not to be pushed aside in our service industry. How do you follow-up with those who phone or email you when you're unable to take their call for one reason or another? Make a decision and make it a discipline to follow up on every phone call, every lead and to answer every email that comes your way as soon as you possibly can. If you don't that will be a sure sign that you've become complacent in your business and your potential client will sense this and find a very quick path to the next salon or mobile therapist on their list.

Think of the times in the past when you've contacted someone and left an enquiry on their phone requesting to be phoned back, or you've been told that so-and-so will return your call shortly or there simply hasn't been any one on the end of the line to take your call. Can you remember how frustrated you felt as time slipped by and no return call; email or acknowledgement came your way. Because you want an answer NOW. How despondent you started to feel about the company or person you contacted because they couldn't be bothered to get in touch because you just weren't important enough, and how your mind starts to wander as you think of other ways to fulfil your needs, wants and desires as another company springs to mind. It can easily happen – you've been there before so don't make the same mistake of putting your clients through the same negative process. You need to do your utmost best to get back to all your enquiries as soon as possible and show them that you are very much interested in them and their enquiry – after all, enquiries with no follow-up means no business.

Now I know some of you may be thinking 'Yeah but I work full-time so I can't physically get back to all enquires as they come in until I get home in the evening, or I'm busy with appointments all day long', well yes I understand this but I'm sure you have short breaks scheduled into your working day where it's possible to check your phone for any missed calls or messages. So in that situation where you have a few moments to spare it's then that you should quickly make an acknowledgement to any client explaining that you're unable to answer their question in full at the moment and to let them know that they will hear from you as soon as you're available which will be in the next 10 minutes, 2 hours or at the end of the day (whichever it may be). This way they will know that you're on the ball and that you're not ignoring them and they'll be happy to wait to hear from you later. They will take satisfaction from the fact that you spared them a short moment of your time. In this fast-paced world that we live in with everyone wanting it NOW, needing it NOW and having answers to their questions NOW – I say Halleluiah for SmartPhones!!

One of the most effective areas of my business is by being totally disciplined every moment in time (where conceivably possible) to answer every email and text message as it comes into my phone, return every message placed on my landline as soon as I can and follow-up with all enquiries at the next available opportunity. People like answers to their questions immediately, they like to be able to make a booking or an appointment right now and they like to know that you care enough about them at this moment in time – they hate to have to wait around for you to get back to them, if you can be bothered to that is. An immediate response will enable you to be in the forefront of securing an appointment before your competitors even have a chance to take breath, and because of this quick response strategy the client is made to feel valued, you become highly regarded as a contentious service provider and before you know it the service is booked. I've had many instances where my prospective customer has returned back to me with comments such as 'Wow that was a fast response, thank you for replying so quickly'. It most definitely works as nine times out of ten I'm able to secure the booking or appointment.

Are You Going The Extra Mile

By being there for them when they need you will reassure your client of your conscious ability and professionalism. You're there when they need you, there to answers questions and there to arrange an appointment with as soon as possible. This will have an overall reflection on the quality of the service that you provide in your beauty business as it will go a long way to enhance your business image, such as being punctual, thorough and considerate.

To go one step further in quality reassurance you could reinforce the conversation with the answers to their questions or notification of an appointment booked by sending them a brief email or text message outlining the details. Again this will accelerate their perception towards you as someone that is truly interested in them and actually takes the time to go the extra mile with exceptional client care. Not only do you need to be as good as you possible can with providing your service, you need to be outstanding with your client care as that will help to enhance your reputation and promote a good-feeling relationship between you. Excellent client care is the cherry on the top of what you do.

Continually striving to improve on what you already do can be achieved by asking your best clients one simple question, "What am I not providing that you would like me to". Listen very carefully on what they have to say and keep an open mind for gaps in the market and niche opportunities. Their answers may leave you feeling a bit taken aback and surprised but those answers will be a primary key in growing your business and building your client relationship. The only opinion that matters is theirs. Aim to please. Is there something that I'm not offering you? What would you like me to provide. Tell me!

Casual conversations can in fact yield something constructive that you may have never discovered unless the conversation had taken place, and you may very well spot something that has been there all along. Discuss with your clients about what they liked about your company, what they didn't like, what they would like you to do differently and what new product or service they would like you to offer. This way you can probe for their un-met needs and desires and any queries that they may have in the general about the industry as a whole. During your time spent with them, and if time and protocol allows, talk to them about any new service launches that are on the horizon and about any new trends that you have seen in the trade magazines, and whether or not it would be something that they may be interested in.

You can get your clients talking by leading them into conversation, but most importantly *listen* to what they have to say. Scrutinize your services regularly and keep asking yourself these important questions:

- What are my clients telling me?
- What are they saying that they want and need?
- What service or product would my clients buy today if I could have offered it to them?
- Are they satisfied?
- Are they loyal to me, and why are they loyal to me?
- Am I reaching my target market successfully?
- How can I improve my service to make it better than before?
- Is my service unique compared to the competition?
- Is my service level selling as I would expect it to?
- Can anyone copy my service and systems identically?

- Have I been presented with an opportunity today through a conversation with a client or through something that I've seen?

Perfection will come over time as long as you continue to ask yourself the above questions and take action with all the answers.

Developing Ongoing Relationships

You may not know it yet but you are sitting on substantial potential that consists of the wealth that is hidden within the care and the relationships that can be built with your clients?

You know the old saying – "It's not what you know, it's who you know". Well that's all very well and good, but how about taking it one step further and thinking about – "It's *what you do* with who you know" – that really matters, and that will make all the difference.

By being genuinely interested in your client is the beginning of the relationship that you should be building with them, and this relationship can last for many years. The more someone likes you the better the relationship will become, and the more they trust you, the more likely they are to book your services or to buy your products again and again. Would you buy from a person that you didn't know, didn't like or didn't trust?

Listen closely when you are having a conversation with your client and by this I don't mean just nodding or shaking your head in conversation and peering over her shoulder at what else is going on. Give good and interesting answers and comments. Make a mental note of anything they say that will help to build your relationship with them and be on the lookout for how you can provide a better experience.

So how can you stand out and be viewed as one of the best and most contentious salons or mobile therapist/stylist there is in your area? Let's look at a couple of ways that you can pull all the stops out.

- On arrival to an appointment give your client a free gift, for no reason at all, just because you care. This could be a reward of some kind – maybe because she's the first client this month or the first person to try out a new range of nail polishes, or because it's her fifth appointment with you.

Gifts could include simple things like a Crispy Crème Donut with a sachet of Hot Chocolate which can be enjoyed during the development process of a hair colour or during a paraffin wax pedicure. Discount coupons from an allied service provider within the industry also make a great gift as does a sample selection of your products. The list is endless of the free and low-cost gifts that you could offer and there are so many ways that you can make a good and lasting impression.

Other gifts that you could use can simply be:

Batch of freshly baked cupcakes
Crispy crème donuts with hot chocolate
Big block of Dairy Milk Chocolate
Mini bubble bath and body lotion
A seasonal pot plant
A big bag of Pick 'n' Mix
A couple of Cinema tickets

When you dig deep and really think about it the list is endless of the low-cost gifts that you can offer as there are so many ways that you can make a good and lasting impression with additional client care which will go a long way to enhance your service provision. It's a nice idea to also gift wrap the items where possible using florists clear paper and curling ribbon to ensure an extra WOW factor.

- Make a mental note on anything they say to you that will help to build your relationship with them. Whatever the info is, write it down at your earliest convenience (could be something interesting happening at their place of work, a holiday they've just had, or their child's tooth that's recently fallen out). You can them drop this into the conversation next time you see them. Your outstanding memory will go a long way and they'll be so impressed that you remembered such a trivial thing. A business owner with a good memory for personal information works a treat.

- Keep a notebook or write on their record card any valuable personal information they may share with you. This could be the names of their spouse, children and pet, their birthday and even small incidental details like where they like to shop.

- Purchase a week-to-a-view diary and keep crucial dates on client information in there such as birthdays including ages, when they first became your client so that it can be recognized and rewarded, keep specific follow-up details such as when they will be returning home from holiday so that you can contact them about booking in for an after-sun conditioning hair and scalp treatment or a luxury body massage to help prolong their suntan. Another good one is to find out about anniversary dates or special evening occasions that they may be attending and contact them to offer any one of your services, such as a French manicure or makeup or a classy hair-up style suitable for the occasion.

- On hearing or reading a story in the newspaper of something of interest about a client of yours, or even through social media, it's a great exercise to follow it up with an email or hand-written note to them to let them know that you saw the article and your specific comments relating to it. I saw an interview on one of my clients children in our local paper that had participated in the Diabetes Fun Run and had raised a vast amount of money for the Charity. I immediately sent her a card to congratulate her on her endeavours. My client was well impressed that I'd actually taken the time and gone out of my way to send her a note congratulating her daughter.

How have you been building relationships with your clients lately?

Client Satisfaction Guaranteed

There are many different ways that you can probe into your client's thoughts about what type of service they are looking for and what they are wanting from you, and a great way to find out is by using a Client Satisfaction Survey on existing clients.

This survey can be done immediately after you have provided your service for them or it can be left with them to complete at their leisure after the service has taken place. It is always a good idea to enclose a pre-paid envelope for them to use if you would like them to post it back, however don't be too disappointed about the response rate as this can sometimes be quite low because they have to make the effort to go to the post-box.

Client Satisfaction Surveys can be produced in all shapes and sizes from the ones where you would ask an open-ended questions and they would write an answer as a short comment, to the ones where you would ask a question that would have a Yes or No answer, to the ones where they score their satisfaction on a scale of 1:10 or on a scale between very satisfied to not at all satisfied. The comment based surveys will also double up as influential social proof and can be used as client testimonials which we'll discuss in a later chapter.

Have a go at designing a Client Satisfaction Survey and list questions like:

You and Your Company
- What they liked about you and your company
- Was your skill in the service what they expected?
- Why they choose you as opposed to another service provider

Your Advertising and Sales Material
- Did an advert you placed play an important role in them booking an appointment with you
- Did they look at your website prior to making an appointment
- Did they book due to a special promotion being offered

The Service You Provided
- Was it value for money
- What did they like about the service you provided for them
- What did they dislike about the service you provided for them
- How likely would they be to re-book the same or similar service.

The Appointment Process
- Were they satisfied with the way the appointment was booked in
- Was the date and time of their choice available
- Were you punctual on arrival if mobile

The After-Sales Process
- Were future needs discussed and advice given
- Was an opportunity for a future appointment made

You could even produce a really simple survey by asking them to make comments on the four things that they liked about your service and the four things that they didn't like. This one works okay but most people feel too embarrassed about writing down their dislikes so tend to leave this box blank which doesn't help if you're trying to make improvements.

So get your thinking cap on and make a list of all the additional care that you can provide your client with. Not only will your excellent care be pleasing to them, you will also get a great sense of satisfaction knowing that you have added value to their lives.

~~~~~

CHAPTER 14

Adding
Immense Value

Stop Selling and Start Giving

In business, as in life, giving is a great experience.

Generally small business owners are so wrapped up in how to increase sales and grow their business in order to improve their own lives that they forget and are missing one essential thing. How are they going to improve and add value to their prospects lives before they even become a client, when they're a client and after the service has been provided or product sold? They need to give, give, give and give more for free. We can become overly immersed in trying to find our next client that we are missing the obvious point here. Start, and start today, thinking about making the life of your prospect easier before they book an appointment for your service or purchase your product and they will be so surprised at how you are different from the masses that they will forever hold you in high esteem. It's a fantastic way of doing business knowing that you are making a big difference to people's lives before they actually part with their money.

We'll take a closer look at each of those three areas – before, during and after sales – and start with the value that we can provide to our client even before we've had the pleasure of servicing them.

Many years ago I was introduced to the giving strategy. I stopped selling to people and started giving to them long before they became customers, by adding value to *their* lives by giving them something that would be useful to them. Being in the creative make-up industry I was able to send them free reports on children's entertainment topics, free contact and resource lists for party planning, free 'How to Run A Stress Free Party' booklet. The list could go on and on. I sent them information in the post, I emailed them and I chatted to them on the phone. It's so true - the more you give the more you get.

The valuable lesson here is that most small business owner's only start giving to their customers and clients after they have parted with their money. It, without a doubt, should be the other way round. You need to start giving to them well before they actually start spending with you.

Can you imagine the look of surprise on your clients face when after an initial telephone enquiry that she made with you she then receives a special report by email specifically geared to her needs. Maybe she's contacted you regarding a facial – so you send her some information on a fabulous skin care range that you use or on a home-care routine she could try out. Maybe she's enquiring about a pedicure, so you can send out a sample of mint enriched foot cream, a routine of foot and ankle exercises to use after a long day of standing and an article written about the effects of ill-fitting shoes and socks. Maybe she's contacted you regarding a new hair style and wanted your advice on cuts – so you can send her some information and photos geared to her specific requirements. Maybe she's a young teen enquiring about prom make-up – so you can send out some photos of make-up designs that will be perfect for her special occasion. The free bundle of information that you send out will be perceived as a welcome bundle of information that she can easily put to use immediately, whether she uses your services in the future or not.

Regardless of your particular niche within the hair and beauty industry there is massive scope for you to devise some free value adding information to your potential clients. So when dealing with enquiries you need to be thinking about how you can provide value to what they want? Devise some questions to ask and rehearse them until they are memorized. Always lead the client by asking the right questions in the right order and of appropriate relevance. You must listen carefully to their answers and on this you can build your 'Value Adding' service from that. Focus on things that are of prime interest to the people you are trying to reach out to and in return make it your goal to help them fulfil their needs before they book an appointment with you.

Even if they don't make an appointment with you during their first point of contact, still offer them a bundle of free information and they'll certainly remember you and the value that you have added for them and you'll come to mind for any future services they may need. Think about it, it's not costing you anything apart from some time in the beginning to make your reports that you can use time and time again, and that client has useful information that you provided for free under no obligation to book your service that she will keep and use to remember you by next time. What a first-class service you are providing!

This is known as Adding Value which is all about going the extra mile and delivering more than the prospective client expects. Consider ways of adding value to your services so that you have an edge over your competitors rather than just competing on price alone. This type of value adding free information can be tweaked to fit in with whatever type of enquiries you may be receiving for any of the services that you provide or the products that you sell – absolutely anything. Regardless as to whether you're a beauty therapist, hair stylist, make-up artist or a nail technician you need think about everything it is that you offer to your clients and compile some sort of free information bundle that compliments the services that you provide. This marketing strategy is a true win-win situation. They win with your free expertise and you'll win their trust.

Start to focus on the fact that the main purpose of your hair or beauty business is to add value to the lives of the people that you come into contact with. Forget about making money and profits, forget about *you* and start thinking about *them* and what they want. Step into their shoes and do whatever it takes to help. Astonish them. Amaze them. Make them feel special. Give them something unanticipated. Cheer up their day. Send them a gift ..... anything that will let them know that you are different from other therapists and stylists and that you genuinely care about them and their needs.

It's also wise to remember that if they don't buy from you this week that doesn't mean that they won't ever buy from you again. People's circumstances change week by week and month by month. Can you remember the leaflet that drops through your letterbox every six weeks from the local estate agent saying that they are short of homes to sell like yours, and to give them a call? I'll bet it goes straight into your waste bin, many, many times over . . . . until one day you decide to move home. Then that little leaflet and the estate agent becomes a service provider that you need to get in contact with immediately and possibly do business with. Everybody's buying situations change on a regular basis. You might not need it today, but someday in the future it may be just what you're looking for. The same scenario as explained above also applies to booking a holiday!

So here's my very strong suggestion to you. Take this concept and seriously think of ways that you can add value to the lives of your clients before they even do business with you. By differentiating yourself from the norm, you will be perceived in a different light, your reputation will soar and people will then be seeking *you* out.

Fulfil their needs by adding additional and immense value to their lives.

Building a Value Adding Service

After you have provided the treatment for your client at her first appointment you have now built up the know, like and trust factor and a relationship of some sort has been started.

You've done the groundwork by adding value to your client's life before they buy and then you've provided your service for them. Then what? You stop in your tracks. You don't bother to telephone them, you don't bother to email them and you don't bother to write to them. They feel abandoned. Shame on you - after such a good start. You see, business doesn't have to stop dead after the service has been supplied or the product has been sold. Far from it in fact. They may feel betrayed that they never hear from you again, that you've forgotten all about them as you haven't kept in contact with them!

You may be thinking to yourself "Well the service that I provide is only going to happen every so often so why bother to keep in touch". That's a very narrow-minded way of thinking as you'll have plenty of occasions to add value to the lives of existing clients. You need to be thinking of new things that you can offer to them, and just as important is to think about the things that you're not yet offering them. You only need to spend as little as an hour a month thinking about a one-off exclusive offer that you can market to your existing client base. It doesn't take that long at all.

If someone has done business with you once they are far more likely to do business with you again. You've probably heard before that it's far easier and cheaper to do business with an existing client than it is to go out and get a brand new one from scratch. Absolutely true. Without regular contact and follow-up with your existing client base you'll lose that opportunity, and with your entire list combined you could stand to lose quite a bit of money. Your aim is to win your clients loyalty for life, to have them buying from you again and again and again, and that will only happen with a value-adding follow-up sequence. Your patience and persistence will pay off to a level that your competitors will not begin to be able to imagine and they are your fastest source to additional monthly profit.

So don't just do business and then ignore them. Send a regular newsletter which is always a great and easy way to stay in touch as the client is still aware of your presence but under no pressure to make an appointment or purchase a product. Don't forget that we're in a creative industry and there is so much information at our fingertips that we can put into a regular newsletter that can be sent to them. Just search the Internet for a specific topic and inform them about your findings and researches.

Keep in close contact by writing to them, emailing them or telephoning them just to show that you care and not necessarily to get an appointment. Alternatively make them an incredible offer with promotions and incentives. Offer them a free gift, or a money off voucher for a referral, and this will give them an enticement as there will be something in it for them. A monthly newsletter is always a great way to stay in touch as the client is still aware of your presence but under no pressure to make an appointment or purchase a product.

Email them a monthly newsletter on things that are happening in the hair and beauty industry. There is plenty of information that you can source from trade magazines and the Internet. Even include topics that aren't directly related to the industry like fashion trends and home-decorating reviews.

- Send out information on hot topics relating to the hair and beauty industry
- Send out information on celebrities who have endorsed the products that you use
- Send out pre-launch information on new products or services that are to hit the industry
- Send out details of your refer and reward scheme that you operate, whereby if your client refers you will reward her with a gift. More on that in another chapter.
- Send out a Costa Coffee voucher on Mother's Day or on her birthday to your best clients or even a

couple of cinema tickets. Give her something totally unexpected that is not connected to your business.

- Send out details of homemade beauty products such as face masks and lip balms.
- Send out information on a competition that you are holding regarding Personal Grooming, whereby the winner with the most enlightening routine will receive a £25 Facial and a spotlight article on your website.
- Send out a personalised hand-written Christmas Card.
- Send them details of your latest service or product and let them know that as a valued client they are privileged to be able to make a future appointment with a 20% - 40% discount.
- Send out a personalised card or email to act as a gentle reminder prior to their next eyelash tint, manicure or hair colour root touch-up.

The list is quite endless when you put your mind to it. Send anything that you can to add value to the life of your client. It doesn't have to cost you the earth and generally it's just your time that you'll be spending – which you'll do once and send out to all your previous clients as once you have put these strategies in place they're so easy to roll out time and time again to everyone. Your follow-up system is important and must be utilized fully on each and every person that has used your service before and it's a good idea to test a selection of sequences that you will be using. Most importantly, don't forget to put some sort of strap-line at the bottom of your mailing to promote you and your business (in a subtle and non-intrusive way of course) and a link that will lead them straight back onto your website.

There will of course be a handful of clients who don't want to hear from you again who will opt-out of your database, and this is quite the norm, so don't get upset or beat yourself up over it. Simply remove them from your list (or your autoresponder will automatically do it for you) and concentrate on those who are happy to hear from you. We'll also be going into more detail about email campaigns later on.

This is the time for you to think about and write down everything that you do now, as standard that adds value to the life of your client that they are paying for. Then you can write down all the additional unpaid things that you do that adds value to their life, which in turn adds perceived value to you and your business. Are their many things that you already do? Next you can write down all the additional value-adding things that you're going to do for them starting from tomorrow and how you're going to implement your new strategies.

Your business will grow so much faster as soon as you understand the importance of adding value to your client's lives. Being in business is not, and should not, be all about making money! You should be filled with a burning desire by making it your goal to add some extra value so you will be perceived in a different light from the norm, and then you will feel an overwhelming sense of achievement knowing that you have truly served your client in every sense of the word. If you are not doing well financially then you are not adding enough value to people's lives. Give your clients what they want and do it better than your competitors are doing it!

So next time, when a client sings your praises, or when a recommendation comes in, or when you receive a letter of thanks in the post - you have done what you set out to do. You have added value to the life of your client, which in turn has certainly added value to your ever-growing business.

~~~~~

CHAPTER 15

Testimonials

Collecting Influential Social Proof

If you've been in business for at least a year you should have at least six good testimonials. If not, why not? How many testimonials did you capture this month, written or verbal, and to what advantage are you using this influential social proof.

Are you making use of the positive things that your client has to say about you? If not, then you need to start compiling a database of testimonials, the powerful written words of others. No matter how much time and effort you have put into the words and sentences of your sales materials, no one says it better about you than how your client says it. Testimonials are perceived as the pure facts about your service or product; they wouldn't make it up, fabricate it or elaborate on the truth like the wordings of an advert may appear to be.

No One Says it Better Than Your Client

Nothing you ever do, nothing you ever say or nothing you ever write about your hair or beauty business will have more impact or power than that of a testimonial from one of your clients. Testimonials, your influential social proof, will be able to communicate the quality of your service far better than you ever can from people who have experienced your service first-hand. And what's more – they're FREE! So how do you go about harnessing that goodwill and accumulating authentic testimonials from your clients? Well simply put - you ASK for them!

Use a guest book (just like those you can buy for Weddings) to capture clients written words. This is an ideal tool as it looks good with its quality cover and has plenty of pages for all you clients to write on, in date order. People can flick through and read what others have had to say about you, and then they can leave their own comments. Nine times out of ten they will add their own testimonial as satisfied clients are only too pleased to provide you with one, so don't be shy about being forthcoming. You should plan to make collecting them an integral part of your business activities, so take your book with you wherever you provide your service and don't forget to leave a pen out!

Testimonials don't just have to be written words either. Another great one is a video testimonial from a satisfied client immediately after you have provided your service to them. Capture the enthusiasm as it happens and add the video to your website, or upload it to Google or to Youtube with a link back to your site. When recording or photographing children, be sure to ask the parent to complete an internet/photographic disclaimer form which will keep you on the right side of the Data Protection Act. For more information on this go to the ICO (Information Commissioners Office) website.

Spontaneous testimonials are also collectable as well. If a client says something in passing or praises you for your work, then ask if you can quote what she has just said in your marketing materials and write it down word for word at your earliest opportunity.

If you have a salon or a dedicated room you should have your testimonials on show, at the ready for your clients to read whilst they are with you. They should be focused on you and your business and the benefits that you can offer them. Have on show scrapbooks of information about your business, what you can offer, what you have achieved and most importantly what your clients are saying about you.

Your best testimonial will be one that gives a detailed description of the service or product that you have provided. This testimonial will go into depth, it will report on your professionalism, your standards, and your value for money and maybe your environment. This testimonial captures all the benefits that you offer, and these benefits will have massive impact and are priceless. During an appointment you could ask your client what feels special about the particular service they are receiving today and how is it benefiting them. If you ask after you have provided your service try questions like how satisfied were they at doing business with you today. The more explicit the comment the better as 'It was great' as an answer won't prove a thing about your competency.

One of the best testimonials you could possibly have is a celebrity endorsement. Hard to come by I know, but well worth pursuing if you can get someone of important statue to use your service and then write an endorsement about it. If you know of a celebrity that lives in your town (even just a C-listed one) you need to follow them on Twitter or Facebook. Start replying to their tweets or posts they make and get into as many conversations as you can with them over a period of time. Eventually you can start dropping little hints in a subtle way during these conversations about the services that you offer. As you gradually build brand recognition, hey-presto they might look to seek you out to arrange an appointment, and there you'll have a celebrity endorsement.

You may find it more comfortable to collect testimonials after the client has had a chance to reflect on the service provided. If this is the case then you could give them a stamped addressed postcard that she can take away with her to complete and send back in to you at a later date. The return of postcards on this type of system can sometimes be quite low though.

If you send a personal thank you email to all of your clients after you have provided your service to them they will probably reply back to you with some sort of comment, appraisal or review about your service which you can then use. After I've provided my face painting training to each and every customer I will send them an email thanking them for using Mimicks as a training provider. Nearly always they will reply thanking me for the course which tends to be accompanied with a fantastic testimonial.

Make sure that all the testimonials you use have the person's permission, or the company's permission to be used in your promotional activities. The full name of the person ideally should be shown along with the town or city in which they are from. Testimonials without this information, especially anonymous ones, will hold no value at all and will be considered made-up and totally useless.

You can never have enough testimonials and you should never stop asking for them. As new ones come in these can replace any that have become a little outdated so that your marketing material is always kept fresh. A clients testimonial will help you to convince people of the promises that you make about your activities, and the words coming from others in the form of a testimonial will most certainly add value to your business. You can further establish your credentials by mentioning other businesses that you've carried out work for.

Go through all your old drawers and cupboards where maybe you have stuffed away some valuable reviews or hand-scribbled notes (that you were going to do something with one day), brush off the dust, and start building your priceless information resources.

- Type out all the testimonials that you already have into a Word Doc in readiness to be pasted into your website
- Purchase a nice guest book and start the ball rolling where you can capture testimonials from your forthcoming clients
- Create a scrapbook of combined information to leave out in your salon for clients to mull over whilst they are waiting for you.

The above task will need time and effort on your part – but once achieved you will have some valuable marketing tools that you can use in many different ways, time and time again. Even if you are just starting out and have no clients yet, provide your service for free to family and friends and then capture the kind words of encouragement that they offer. These testimonials will start you off quite nicely.

Use your testimonials anywhere and everywhere your prospective client will be looking, including your advertising, your sales literature, your display banner and even on your t-shirt or tunic! Use short phrased ones on your business cards and use a wealth of your longer phrased ones throughout the pages of your website. In fact everywhere and anywhere that you know your prospective client will be looking. Take a look at any of the Mimicks Websites and you'll see testimonials in abundance, working their magic! So go for it, start collecting them today or retrieve those that you have stuffed away in a drawer somewhere, and use them everywhere you possibly can!

Make better use of your testimonials – you worked hard for them, so put them absolutely everywhere.

~~~~~

CHAPTER 16

Marketing Your Business

Get Yourself Out There Big Time

Marketing – quite a scary word, don't you think?

The very mere thought of marketing your hair or beauty business can give you brain frieze, just like when you eat your favourite ice cream – pleasure from the results but it can be a very painful experience getting there! For some, the thought of how to successfully market their business can turn their legs to jelly and put a knot in their stomach. Maybe you're one of those reluctant marketers too, worrying about what others may think of you. If so, you need to reframe how you view your marketing strategies because if you're in business then your clients need you and they need to know how to get hold of you. Remember that you do the job you do, to help others and to effectively solve their problems.

The businesses I have run over the years have been using many profitable marketing tactics and this section of the book is dedicated to revealing the success stories, the tactics and the systems that made my companies successful in every way possible. I've learned and developed some sound concepts and special techniques that are easily transferable from my business straight into yours and hopefully I'm going to shine a brighter light for you to follow in all your marketing endeavours. There are many sources of marketing out there that you could use, and whether you choose to take and put into practice the information that I can provide for you, or you choose another source of provider – the bottom line is - *are you going to make it happen?* So over the next few chapters we'll take a look at how to make your inspirational ideas really stick, and turn your fears of marketing into the supporting success story of *your* business, which will leave your competitors still standing in the ice-cream queue!

If you want to attract more clients so that they can book your services – then they need to know that you're out there waiting for their business. You need to get yourself 'out there' by actively marketing your business, big time. Big time!

Firstly you need to remember that providing your service is not the priority in your business as it's all about the marketing of your service, which is your fastest way to wealth. So stop being just a beauty therapist or make-up artist and become the marketer of your business as well. That's the big difference between earning just enough pocket-money to get by to actually earning substantial sums from your venture. You need to put as much focus into your marketing plan in order to get more clients to experience what you do rather than spending all your energy just on the tools. So put your beauty kit down and concentrate ON where the money is coming from.

If you change your mindset and start to work ON your business rather than IN your business by introducing new marketing systems and seeing them through then your business growth will soar. I have built up many of my businesses by using this strategy – in the beginning I was always the chief cook and bottle washer, and over time employees were hired to lessen my load, and with my load lessened the businesses grew as I was able to commit more time *on* the business. I took myself off the tools full-time which enabled me to put plans into action, accomplish new ideas and implement new services or bring in new retail products. Soon it could be time for you to hand over the tools of the trade for some of your appointments to someone else (even if in the beginning it was only a few here and there) and time for you to take control of the reigns and push your business in the direction of success with a sound marketing plan. Remember - it's not all about doing your thing, it's all about marketing your thing!

Marketing is Like Gardening

Before we get going with this chapter you need to remember that Marketing is the same as Gardening:

- In gardening you plant a seed with expectations of growth. In marketing you plan a strategy to implement with expectations of growth.
- In gardening you water that seed to promote growth and in marketing you keep adding more ideas into the mix to promote growth.
- In gardening you remove some shoots to help the plant expand and develop further. In marketing you remove a few ineffective tactics in order to concentrate on the more effective ones.
- In gardening there comes a time when that baby plant needs to be re-potted because it's outgrown its original one, so you find a bigger pot. In marketing those first initial small ideas you once had are growing very successfully so you now need to expand with your software, design a bigger and better website or maybe move into premises.
- Your baby seedling has now turned into a magnificent plant through the love and care that you enriched it with. It gives you much pleasure knowing that you gave it life and the people who see it admire your skill and expertise. Your business has grown from that initial thought into an

outstanding company and you feel very proud of your endeavours and your clients hold you in high-regard because they know that you care about them.

- In gardening if you don't continue to feed and water your plant it will stop blossoming, it will become dehydrated, crinkle up and it will die. That's your fault. Not the environments fault, the economy's fault, your partners fault or the plants fault. It's your fault, because you just didn't care enough. In marketing if you don't continue to nurture your ideas, implement your strategies, build client relationships, expand your business principles, look for opportunities to exploit, promote yourself with a vengeance – well in a nut-shell your business will die. That's your fault. Not the environments fault, the economy's fault, the banks fault, your competitors fault, the industry's fault. It's your fault, because you just didn't care enough. People with unsuccessful businesses are always so quick to blame other people and other situations for their downfall, they never once stop to think to themselves 'Well maybe it's my fault that my business collapsed'!

So as you can see marketing is so like gardening – when things are looking good it's all because you have made it possible, and made it happen and when things are looking bad it's a reflection of your actions, or lack of actions that caused the whole thing to shrivel up and die! Go and buy a pack of plant seeds and you'll see what I mean.

Secret Services and Private Products

If you've got the expertise, the talent and the goods that people want and need but have little or no self-promotion, how are your potential clients going to find out about you? It's your duty as a small business owner to get out there and promote your services or product to as many people as you can or else you run the risk of depriving someone of your solution to their problem! If your intention in business is to be successful, and I'm absolutely sure it is - you need to be drawn towards that main sense of purpose. Having energy and determination with your marketing, how you connect with new clients or reconnect with existing ones, is a necessity for your future accomplishment.

You're in business, so remember to show off. Think of your business as an extension of who you. You should be strutting your stuff and blowing your own trumpet, as loud as you possibly can, as you'll do yourself no favours by having a secret service or a private product (what's the point of that). Get out there and market yourself to the masses because unfortunately no-one else is going to do it for you.

A lot of small business owners hate the thought of self-promotion in the fear of being too pushy and too 'in ya face' when it comes to marketing, as any rejections they incur could be felt on a personal level. How many times have you walked past someone doing market research in the street and you've said "No thank you" to them when they try to encourage you to stop. They get rejection after rejection after rejection, but they still keep going with a smile on their face. They know that they'll have to hear those formidable words 'No thank you' many, many times before they will manage to hook someone who is willing to stop and give them their time and say 'Yes'. The same thing will apply to your business marketing as you'll need to be persistent, you'll need to be alert and you'll most certainly need to feel confident in your self-promotion because eventually someone will say yes to your phone call, or your advert or your mail-shot. So don't hide away in the dark and expect your clients to find you, because they won't. If you want more business, you have to go after it at full force.

Struggling business owners who are feeling the pinch and just about making ends meet will glaze over when they hear the word marketing. They're the ones who tend to carry on as they always have, getting what they've always got – which will inevitably be a struggling business. You know the old saying "If you always do what you've always done, you'll always get what you've always got". I'll repeat that – If you always do what you've always done, you'll always get what you've always got. I hear business owners complaining about how slow business is, and not many bookings, appointments or sales lined up, and when I ask how they are promoting themselves they say "Oh just the usual way of advertising". They're standing still and not moving the business forward to a higher level by becoming *outstanding* in their marketing. A handful of leaflets here and there or an isolated newspaper advert is not going to make a thriving business. Successful business owners on the other-hand will light up when they hear the word marketing as they understand its purpose and its importance for creating wealth and putting money in the bank. Unfortunately, without marketing in any shape or form, your business ain't going nowhere sunshine!

By making a decision and laying down a discipline and agreeing to yourself that **once a week** you will endeavour to do **one marketing activity** within your business that in turn will make money, will be a huge step in the right direction. There are so many different ways that you can sell your service or promote your product to potential customers and clients but you will need to put the same amount of conviction and passion into developing at least one new marketing activity each week like you do when you are actually providing your service.

So where to start – well here's a little helping hand of some of the procedures that you could be using, which I'll be going through in more detail soon.

You'll need to get yourself a good marketing mix that should include some, if not all of the following:

1. **Advertising:** What are you already doing? Scrutinise it. Are you doing influential direct response adverts with grabbing headlines and persuasive call to actions which produce clear measurable results which makes the reader ready to do business with you? Do you know the cost of conversion for each advert and your ROI (return on investment)?
2. **Direct Mail:** Do you know your demographics inside out and where to find and reach your target market?
3. **Your Website:** Is it working hard enough for you or is it in need of a major workout? How good are your search engine rankings? Are all your tags installed effectively? Are you tracking and

analysing your site visitors and do you know how many are converting to paying clients?

4. **Email Campaigns:** Are you building relationships with your clients and sending them value-adding information on a regular basis in the form of a regular newsletter or blog.

5. **Telephone:** Do you routinely spend time on the phone to your clients to increase your revenue and maximise your earning potential?

6. **Press Releases:** Are you exposing your business to the National and local media in order to position yourself as an expert in the industry?

7. **Alliances:** Who is in your gang and who else would you like to be in your gang?

8. **Referrals:** Are you getting enough of them and if so how are you rewarding the referring client?

Now be honest with yourself - how many of the above do you systematically use to entice your clients to use your hair or beauty service?

Maybe at this point you're thinking "Yeah, but all this marketing stuff costs a great deal of money". Well let me tell you that that's where you're so very wrong, and I'd like to dispel that illusion. There are many ways that you can market your business successfully without breaking the bank to do so. If you have a low budget then there are low-cost strategies for you to use and some are even free and you'll only need to be testing in order to find the ones that work out for you. What you'll need to be spending though is time, and sometimes plenty of it. The time and persistence spent on your marketing activities will show a great return and more profitable income streams. So are you going to make that informed decision to take action with your marketing? I hope so, as there is probably so much untapped potential in your business which can be yours if you're prepared to work hard for it.

Now on the other hand you might be saying here that business is plentiful, can't book another appointment, you are already a supreme marketer, and all that jazz. That's great - but did you know that as good as your business is, every aspect of your business still has room for improvement and then it should be improved again. After your improvements have been made you should immediately start looking to improve them once more. Don't stand still and don't ever become complacent. Take a long critical look at all your systems and how you operate, and always have an open mind to new opportunities for taking your business one step further. If you are fully booked and can't possibly take on any new business, then the obvious answer here is it's time to recruit and train more staff to take you to the next level. That's what happened to me in my business over twenty years ago

– so I took on extra staff to help with the demand of bookings that were coming in. I trained them up to our standards and they were then able to attend events on behalf of the company. It was not unusual during the high season summer months to have six events running in one day covered. All that only happened because I made a decision to make it happen.

Set Yourself a Marketing Plan

So how do you initially get yourself going with this 'marketing thingy' and propel yourself into the same league like the big guys? The one and only answer is to become a master marketer – it really is as simple as that! You need to try out as many marketing activities as you can for your business – but remember, always on a small scale first. Also don't put all of your eggs into one basket at the same time and your energy into one marketing element because if it's no good and it flops then that will be a whole lot of wasted time. You need to be testing a variety of things all at once. If a particular campaign was successful, keep doing it, and each time roll it out on a bigger scale.

Before you set your marketing plan into action you need to ask yourself some simple questions:

- What sets you apart from your competitor that makes you unique from them? Are you different? How are you different?
- Are you clearly communicating all the benefits of your service to your clients, Do they know how you're going to add value to their lives?
- Do you copycat what your competitors do with regards to advertising, promotion and pricing? If it's good enough for them, is it good enough for you. Really? Or are you wasting money just like them?
- Does your current advertising make the reader eager to do business with you? Do you know the cost of conversion from the adverts that you place?

How did you answer? Were you able to answer? Do you feel that you're ready for a change in the way you market to your client?

A really great marketing exercise to do is to critically analyze your working environment if you are fortunate enough to have a salon. Is everything you see around you geared to help and aid with your selling process? Is it marketing to your client? Do you have promotional material on view for them to look at as they wait for their appointment? I hope so.

With that in mind, think about the time you've been waiting for an appointment at the Doctor's, the Dentist's, the MOT place or the pizza shop. What do they have on offer for you to read as you wait? Magazines, plenty of magazines. Why are they filling your mind with irrelevant information that isn't about them and their business and what they can offer to you, their customer or client? Waiting areas should be filled with positive information about the company - portfolios of photographs, case studies, testimonials and letters from customers and suppliers and even certificates of achievement. When people are in your establishment, your area so to speak, you don't want them to be doing anything else other that looking and reading about what you do, the benefits your service has to offer them and being communicated to in a way that motivates them into making an enquiry, or booking an appointment for that amazing service of yours that they've just read all about or a purchase a product of some sort.

Before we get onto the 'where to advertise' in the next few chapters let's get onto the 'how to advertise'. Your advert, regardless of whether it's in a community magazine, information on your website, or on the back of a bus, must be clear to the reader about what it is you want them to do. So what do you want them to do? You want them to contact you of course. Easy. If they don't telephone you, email you, text you, or write to you as soon as they see your advert – they are very unlikely to do business with you and become your client. So that's your main point for placing an advert, any advert whether it's offline or online, to get those prospective clients to get in touch with you now_so they can hear all about what it is that you have to offer them.

Attention Grabbing Headlines

So first things first – the headline. This is essential to get right when designing your adverts as this could be the make or break with regards to your potential client reading on. You want your headline to entice them in so that they continue to read the rest of the advert, right through the copy, right down to the call to action. If you've got your call to action just perfect your client may not even get that far if you've got a lousy headline. People are in a hurry these days and most just scan adverts in newspapers and magazines, only reading the headline, and if the headline isn't screaming benefits, benefits, benefits then their eyes will wander on to the next advert in view and yours will be long gone I'm afraid.

Good headlines will make your reader curious to know more. You could start with an announcement for something new in the hair or beauty industry. Your headline could ask the reader a question like 'What if ....' and get them to mentally answer it. Another good headline is the 'How to' headline. People like being told how to do certain things in a certain way, especially if it's going to make their life easier. Remember that the main purpose of your headline is to get the readers to read on through the rest of your advert.

So what's an example of a boring headline?
- Pedicure for Your Summer Holiday

A much better example of the same headline:
- Are Your Feet Ready? With Summer just round the corner your feet need to be ready for your strappy sandals. Treat yourself to a luxury pedicure that includes a skin polish massage with toenails that are painted to perfection (the customer sees a picture in their mind).

Make your headlines so interesting that your reader will be compelled to read on. Your titles should be about how to overcome something. It needs to grab attention. It needs to answer the question "What's in it for me".

Below is a list of a dozen headlines that would have massive impact in your advertising:

- The 5 Steps to Selecting a Great Hair Stylist (and then list them)
- Discover How to .... so that you never have to............... (could be about how to apply long-lasting foundation)
- The 6 ways you can benefit from ......(having a mobile therapist/stylist come to you)
- What Do You Like (Need, Love, Hate) The Most (Least, Worst, Best) About Visiting The Hairdressers [list the benefits, reasons, challenges]
- We're very excited about .....[launch something new/review something that is topical in the news that is relevant to the hair and beauty industry]
- Hot Off The Press. Discover our brand spanking new ....[a new service/a new product]
- If You've Been Searching (Looking) For .... Then We Have The Answer [the benefits of making an appointment with you]
- This Seasons Trends in Nail Art is ..... [list them]
- There's More Than One Way to Apply Your make-up for your (Wedding, special occasion, party) [tell them what it is]

Try using power words in your headlines such as:

Compelling, Crucial, Essential, Explosive, Fantastic, Impact, Massive, Revealed, Eliminate, Secret, Smart, Presenting, Introducing, Eliminate, Abolish, Remove, Reduce, Discover, Find Out, Learn, Realise, Uncover, New, Innovative, Fresh, Recent, Latest, Modern.

Have a go at writing fifty different headlines, yes fifty and decide on the single best one. Make them striking, interesting, attention grabbing and thought provoking. Don't throw the others away though as these can be stored in a file to pull out and use as inspiration another day. On one occasion it took four hours for my husband and me to write the headline of a single press release because we wanted to get it just right. In your file also keep cutting examples of other headlines that people have used that you can pull out for motivation.

Copy Writing –
not to be confused with Copy Right!

The words you write whether on an advert, on your posters and other sales material or on your website must persuade the reader to get in contact with you. It's all about taking the reader through a journey of powerful evoking word pictures that shows them how their life would be easier, improved, complete, productive, fulfilled or whatever if they did business with you. Your service may help them to save time, save money or save worrying. Write your copy so that it resonates with the reader, write in the way that they would write and keep a conversation tone going rather than a formal editorial piece which may be off-putting to them.

It's true, the copy in your adverts should contain AIDA (get their Attention, make them Interested, give them a Desire to buy from you and then finally give them the Action they need to do to contact you) but it goes a lot further than that. Your copy should sell the end result, sell the benefit and above all sell the emotion. Statistics show that all buying decisions are 80% emotional – how it'll make the consumer feel.

People are so busy these days and are faced with information overload wherever they look. So much information at their fingertips, too much information to take in all at once. We have all become conditioned to scan-read, skipping through big chunks of text for isolated words that are beneficial to us, that resonate with us, that will give us what we're looking for. Your words that you write need to jump out from the page, they need to make the reader stop in their tracks and take time to actually read the full paragraph or advert. So make sure you put the crucial piece of information first that you want to get across to them because if you take a long time getting to the point with too much waffle you'll lose the readers interest in a flash. Keep sentences short as well and use bullet points that are easily read and picked out.

Some good advice and tips on copy writing are:

- Be the prospective client reading your copy. Does it meet *your* needs, is it what *you* desire, will it fulfil *your* dreams?
- Make the copy simple to read. Don't complicate it with technical jargon or complicated language. Write in conversation tone, as you would speak as if chatting with a friend, using correct grammar and spelling though – not the type you see in text-talk.
- Place the focal point on the benefits and make the features a minimal comparison. When you book the guy to come in and clean your oven, you're not interested in what brilliant cleaning chemicals he uses, you're just interested in how clean your cooker will look so you won't be embarrassed when you have the family round for dinner. Think benefit, benefit, and benefit.

Two hugely powerful words to include in your copy writing is the words You and Your. Make your copy all about them and not just anybody. Open up your webpage now, or a handful of other peoples hair or beauty sites, and you'll find that the majority will be over cramming their site with sentences that start with 'We can do this' or 'We will do that' or 'We have this'. Pages are filled with the word we, we, we. The customer or client doesn't care about you, that word is not about the them, it's about the company. Take a long serious look at the copy that you've written and anywhere that it says 'We' change and tweak it to the word You or Your, and make it all about them.

Direct Response Advertising

Okay, so they've read your attention grabbing headline and the content you've written has kept them reading on, next you need to stimulate a response from them, for without a direct response it will be a waste of a good advert and quite unlikely that they will ever become your client. How many times have you seen an advert for something you'd like, you tear the advert out of the newspaper/magazine, you put the torn piece of paper on the sideboard, in your handbag, on the fridge – and then what? You forget to contact them, you can't be bothered anymore to contact them, and your fleeting desire has passed. The advert stays there for a few weeks gathering dust and then it goes in the bin! Wasted opportunity – the seller didn't make that advert compelling enough for you to contact them immediately so that a sale could be made.

Now the direct response that you want to receive from them can actually be a number of things. Do you want them to contact you for a brochure, do you want them to visit your website, do you want them to make an appointment right now, do you want them to receive a free gift or to come along to a service launch party. You could write a special report about something you are most passionate about within the industry, and use that as a giveaway to anyone that contacts you. There are numerous reasons that you may wish for your client to get in touch with you – and remember that the more appealing the offer, the more likely it is that they will get in touch (especially if you're offering a free gift, sample or report, etc).

Your direct response can also be for an offer that has a specific deadline, something that needs to be purchased or booked this week or by the end of the month. People move much quicker if you put the scarcity factor into place by letting them know that once it's gone it's gone. Have you purchased something because you've been told there's only so many left, only a few more days remaining to get it at this price or only a limited edition? I bet you have at some time.

After placing your advert and on your client contacting you it's essential for you to capture their full information, with their permission for future marketing purposes of course. You will need their details so that you can add them to your growing base of potential clients, and then with this information it can be used over time to build a relationship with them by informing them about your products, services, special promotions and packages that you offer. It's all about building relationships with people and not just trying to sell to them in the first instance. It's worth noting here again that people buy from who they like, know and trust rather than buying cold from an isolated advert. It's wise to put some sort of system in place here for asking people who contact you where they heard about you from. You may have multiple adverts running at one time, or leaflets being picked up at various points, or posters displayed out there in the community, so you'll need to know where the interest is coming from. Devise some sort of document whereby you can capture this information by simply asking "Can I ask where you heard about me from" and log it immediately. Just a simple A4 sheet with your marketing headings written across the top (advert, leaflet, poster, etc) with columns for you to write the client information in will be all that's needed for you to effectively gauge the responses as they come in.

Keep on track of your sums as well and know how many responses you'll need in order for them to turn into actual clients. Just because you get say ten responses that may not make the cost of the advert worthwhile unless a couple of those responses generates into an appointment, and the net profit from those clients are equal to the cost of the advert or is much greater than the cost of the advert. This is where testing (more on this in a moment) plays an important role in your marketing. Test all of your marketing activities on a regular basis – and if it's working then keep on doing it.

Make sure your adverts are influential direct response adverts, as they will produce clear measurable results. Also bear in mind that too much useless information crammed into your adverts or other sales material could inadvertently bombard your customer with visual whiplash. So keep it simple.

The Call to Action

With your direct response advert in place you must let the client know *how* to contact you, for without it they will be confused and you will end up losing their interest. So a direct response advert means letting them know how to contact you right now, yep right now. You might want them to telephone you, to email you, or to go to your website and submit a sign-up form, to name but a few. This is called the 'call to action and is generally found at the bottom of an advert. Whatever is your chosen method, make sure that it is clear and direct about what they need to do, when you want them to do it, and why you want them to do it and of course what's in it for them.

You could put deadlines in your call to action so that people have something to work with. Your offer may be just for the coming weekend or must be used by the end of a particular month, or you could state that you only have xyz left and it goes to the first twenty callers.

By designing your adverts with a direct response in them and a call to action, will automatically give you the evidence as to whether the advert is working or not. No responses will indicate that it was a waste of money because no-one called, compared to a good response of callers meaning that it could potentially be money well spent.

A Load of Old Nonsense

Take a moment here to reflect on how your clients come to you. Was your first thought - "Well I advertise in the local newspaper, or in the local directory, or in the Yellow Pages? That's where my competitors advertise as well and it brings in most of my business". Well let me tell you - don't believe that when you have a business you have to advertise in countless newspapers and magazines in order to be successful. Not only is most paper advertising a waste of time but it will also be very demoralizing for you, as you will feel that your business is worthless if you don't get the response or appointments that you expected. Just because your competitor advertises in a certain publication it certainly doesn't mean that you should as well. Have they been testing and measuring the response of that advert to discover whether or not it is really working for them. Probably not! So don't copy them.

Think about the most recent advert that you placed in any publication. Can you see it in your minds-eye? Where in the publication was it placed? Was it easy to find? Did it jump out from the rest? How many enquiries did you get from that advert and how many appointments were made? What was the client conversion rate? I'll take a guess here that you don't exactly know! Don't worry though, as most business owners haven't got a clue whether their advertising is working or not! You need also to remember that conversion rates in your marketing can be lower than expected, but when you do secure a new client they can be worth their weight in gold to you and far outweigh the cost it took to get them in the first place.

To find out for certain how well your adverts are doing, as well as all your other marketing activities, you must TEST and MEASURE all aspects of your advertising campaigns – regularly, without fail.

Testing the Effectiveness of Your Marketing

Never be fooled by placing an advert in a publication and leaving it to run for a couple of months in the hope that it will work. Keep track of it, regularly.

You need to consistently know:

- How many direct responses were made
- How many of those turned into actual clients
- How much income was generated from those clients

- What could the lifetime value of each client be worth
- If the profits were greater than the cost of the advert

If any of your advertising isn't working, you must stop the advert immediately. Just by prolonging it by keeping it going isn't going to mean that eventually it will take off because it won't. If it's not working for you now, then it's very unlikely that it won't work at all. Ever! This is a big trap that a lot of business owners fall into. They are under the illusion that to be advertising is a good thing to be doing with no regard as to how efficient that little advert really is. You must, must, must get into the habit of testing and measuring the responses and results of your advertising and make a quick, quick, quick decision as to whether it's viable to carry it onwards and upwards or whether to cut your losses and quit before you waste another whole load of hard-earned money.

Draw out some sort of table matrix that you can use to record all the elements of your advert and stick to tracking the information as it happens. This will provide valuable information for you and will help you to plan any future paper-based advertising campaigns.

The things that you'll need to record on your matrix will be along the lines of:

- The publication *(Village Newsletter)*
- Its verification readership *(1270)*
- The cost of advert *(£98.00)*
- The duration of the advert *(one month)*
- How many other similar advertisers like you *(4)*
- Page number advert placed *(5)*
- Position of advert on page *(top right corner)*
- Colour or black and white *(colour)*

And now for the most important elements to be tested and measured are:

- Your Headline - *what it said*
- Your Copy Writing - *what it read*
- Your Direct Response - *what it was*
- Your Call to Action - *what was used*
- How many enquiries did you receive
- What follow-up process you used
- How many appointments were made

You should also test different page positions as you'll find that adverts placed on the right hand page tend to be looked at and read more so than those on the left hand page. Even better is to get your advert on the right hand page in the right hand corner. Change the colour and style of your fonts every now and then and use different photos or graphics, or don't use photos or graphics at all. But make sure that you test and record the different ways that you are doing things.

To get a better understanding of your adverts you need to try different publications and different media sources. Try your adverts out on a small-scale basis though, and certainly don't agree to long successive adverts running in one single publication unless you are sure that it is a dead cert and will bring you in a definite return on investment. Speaking of long-term adverts it is imperative that you get your Yellow Pages advert 100% perfect if that's where or you choose to advertise as it's there for a very long time and unchangeable over the duration. I once had a Yellow Pages advert that was the wrong colour shade or red (too much orange) unlike my known branding then, and unfortunately I was stuck with it for twelve months! Times have really changed over the past decade as the Yellow Pages is no longer a place where I advertise anymore.

By continually testing, recording and measuring each and every advert along with each and every element of the advert will give you a better understanding of what is working and what isn't. Change and tweak your adverts on a regular basis and you'll get a clearer picture of what works and what doesn't. Ditch the ones that are not working hard enough for your money.

- Change things like the headline, and compare to a previous advert.
- Change things like the page placement, and compare.
- Change things like the copy, and compare.
- Change things like the direct response message, and compare.
- Change things like the call to action, and compare.

Don't keep running the same old boring advert that you have been doing for months (or even years) just because it is easy to do so, just because it's less hassle to update, and just because your competitors do! Change it and change it as often as possible (obviously not possible for the yellow pages, however your free listing on yell.com can easily be changed often and is well worth doing).

If you test and measure a couple of new marketing strategies each month on a small scale basis, say twenty-four over the year, at the end of that time you should have at least a dozen or so that you know are working, which you can continue with on an ongoing basis and that will be sufficient enough for you to turn your business around. Believe me – it works. You need to be doing many marketing activities all at once and not just paper-based advertising, and testing, measuring and recording the results on each and every one of them. If what you're doing is working and it turns out that you made money, even if it's only a small amount then you need to roll it out on a bigger scale again and again. You must be in a position that you know how much each marketing activity is costing you, how much revenue it's producing and of course how much profit it will make. Likewise stop anything that isn't working.

So to recap – test on a small-scale basis and measure the response. If you made a good return on investment, roll it out again, and again. If it's not – you know what to do!

So with that said, let's get straight on to some great little marketing strategies that I've used on my businesses over the next couple of chapters ....

~~~~~~

CHAPTER 17

Advertising Offline

Where To Advertise

We've spent some time looking at how to advertise by using effective direct responses, call to actions and compelling headlines that can be used across the board in all of your sales literature and promotional material. Now it's time to look at *where* to advertise, what different business building principles you can use and how to best market yourself.

Newspapers

You probably have a local newspaper that covers your immediate area and this is a great place to try out paper-based advertising. Give the editor a telephone call to find out if there is a forthcoming feature being run on the hair or beauty industry, or ask if there is some kind of advertorial that can be run about you, which is a combination of you placing an advert with the publication and them writing some editorial about you.

And don't forget you must remember to make it a direct response advert with a compelling call to action for the prospective client to make as you will be competing against many, many other advertisers that evening and your advert must stand out from the rest to be in with a chance (remember chip-paper tomorrow)!

There are a number of low-cost publications that you can test the water with, and it's far better to build your advertising up slowly and steadily than to go in at full force and spend your entire marketing budget on just this one strategy alone as there are so many other ones to choose from.

I don't particularly like newspaper advertising because it's expensive and you're in competition with too much other stuff which is a barrier to your advert actually being seen. However it does tend to have a huge reach – but not necessarily to the right target market, yours.

Community Magazines and School Newsletters

Find out if your local neighbourhood has a community magazine – the sort that comes out monthly and covers a widespread area in your location. This type of community magazine tends to stay around on home-owners coffee tables for a while and over the month may be picked up and casually glanced at many, many times, unlike a newspaper that is here today and gone tomorrow.

Contact some of the other trades that advertise in it to get a feel for what you could expect from the publication and find out if they're securing new customers and clients from their advert.

You may again also enquire if the editor of the magazine is interested in doing a piece about you as a feature to go alongside your advert which will go a long way towards your business profile, especially if you're new to the industry. Maybe offer her a free service so that she can report back on it in the community magazine.

Direct Mail Shots

Traditional direct mail is a bundle of information that you send out to your existing clients or potential clients in the post over a period of time. This can be in the form of a postcard, to a leaflet or brochure to a long sales letter. Either way it's a sales message that you are sending out to a specific group of people. To run a successful direct mail campaign you must send multiple postings to your client in order for them to sit up and take note. An isolated postcard in the post to them from you outlining any special offers that you're promoting this month has every likelihood of going straight into the waste bin. However if you take time to seriously think about the sequence of your campaign and what you intend to send to your client over the next two, three and four months you stand a better chance of conversion as it has all been carefully planned out.

The hard truth about direct mail shots is that about 90% of your mailings will go in the bin, but (and here's the best bit) that also means that 10% won't. And out of that 10% (say ten people) a few may only glance at it, a few may read it and a few may respond to it. Now that may seem quite low but it could in fact be a very profitable direct marketing campaign. Its' not down to how many responses you get it's down to whether the quantity of responses were profitable or not. Always test and measure against profit made. That one client who makes an appointment for your service may far out-weigh the cost of the letter and postage to the whole group you sent out to especially if you are in a position to be able to calculate their life-time value to you.

You should always embark on a direct mail campaign on a small scale basis first. Invest only an amount of money that if it didn't work out it would be no big deal to lose, but at the same time large enough to be able to get a couple responses from it. If your small-scale direct mailing has worked then roll it out again and again and increase its size along the way as you continue to do so.

Leaflet Drops

Your leaflets can be placed at many locations in your community such as allied hair or beauty service providers, nursery schools, gymnasiums, health clubs and public houses to name but a few. It's a nice idea to provide the company that has agreed to display your leaflets with a counter-top Perspex holder for your leaflets to go in as they are less likely to throw your marketing material away if you have gone to this sort of trouble. However, on your next visit to re-stock you may find that it is gathering dust in a corner somewhere – this is the chance you'll have to take!

Posters

Have a go at placing posters in libraries, community centres and recreation clubs. You may even find that local independent shops and stores in your neighbourhood would be happy to promote you, especially if you can make it worth their while with a gift voucher, a value adding plan or referral system (which we'll discuss later).

Postcards

Your local mini supermarket and Post Office will more than likely have a customer notice board where people advertise their unwanted items for sale on postcards. Another great and really cheap place for self promotion. Stick a photo of one of your services on the card as well.

Banners and A Frames

If you have a salon or salon space the big free-standing promotional banners have really come down in price recently and they are a great form of advertising your services. You can put a vast amount of written information on them along with some photographic evidence of your service provision.

Your Uniform

The uniform that you wear whether it's a t-shirt or tunic is one of the best places for you to advertise. Your uniform doesn't just have to have your business name on it as it is a prime space to have a special promotion printed on. This could go along the lines of 'We're providing FREE NAIL ART to every client who books an appointment for a set of extensions next month'.

SHERRILL CHURCH

You could go one step further by having a call to action printed on that says 'Book your appointment today for a 10% discount'. A good statement which has a huge benefit to the client – something that's free and at a discount. This t-shirt or tunic can be worn at any time and is always applicable to the following month.

Your Car or Van

As you travel here and there you will be more highly regarded in your community as a hair or beauty service provider if you have your company details sign-written onto your car. You probably see it time and time again where you live – builders, florists, gardeners and electricians to name but a few professions will use this form of advertising to get them known around their area. You might not need a gas installer at the moment but the day that your boiler breaks down is the day you say 'Oh yeah, there's that guy I see quite often driving around, I'll call him'.

Make the advertising on your car benefit focused so that you are offering something of value to your potential client. Bullet points of what you do are very ineffective unless you have a benefit attached to each one on how it can enhance the life of your client. Take a look at the sign-written cars and vans as you drive around and reflect on the words that they use, what is the benefit to you, is there one? You'll probably realise here that 99% have no benefits whatsoever, plenty of bullet points, but no benefits written at all!

Raffle Prizes

Most schools holding their summer or winter fete, and even the local village committee, are on the lookout for free gifts from local businesses to add to their raffle as a prize. Choose a handful of local events and offer a special Raffle Prize to include a free service. Make sure you have terms and conditions in place as you wouldn't want the winner to live two hours away if you are offering a mobile service! This strategy is also a sure-fire way to get into the school's brochure and advertising.

When I had my Fairytale Children's Party Venue a couple of years ago, we always had a Christmas Grotto and countless schools, nurseries and charities asked for donations of free entry tickets to be entered into their raffles or draws. We found that by giving away one free child's ticket per school the winner of the prize would invariably want to bring along their other children so they would purchase additional tickets to suit their needs. A great and effective way to advertise your business and to generate more income. A win-

win situation. So even though you may well be giving away something for nothing there is always the chance that this person could indeed become a regular client.

Telephone

Your telephone conversations with your clients should grab their attention and be creative. When making telephone calls remember to introduce yourself and state your reason for calling. Use the clients name where applicable and listen to their needs and let them talk, regardless of whether you're making the call to the them or whether they're contacting you. Have some sort of script at the ready that you can follow in order to ask the right questions and gauge their responses (however make sure you don't sound like your reading it out in parrot fashion as I'm sure you know how that sounds if someone rattles off a written script). Work out a sequence script for all of your calls and jot down bullet points for your lead conversation. This script can then be typed out and kept in readiness to go through as contact is made.

You could also try this one out. Randomly contact five recent clients by telephone as a courtesy and ask how they enjoyed your service that you provided for them. Find out if you could make any improvements to make the experience better and if they felt that anything was missing from the service. Ask for as much feedback as possible. Don't attempt to sell them anything, nothing at all. By giving excellent client care you will immediately add value to them and to your business. If you're able to get one out of the five to re-book you without even trying – then that indeed was a great exercise. How much more revenue would that mean to your business if you routinely telephoned all your clients after all their appointments?

Always remember to test your phone campaigns. Test the time of day that you make the call and also test the day of the week. You could always record yourself to check whether you were clear enough, did you sound too pushy, did you sound generally interested in your clients needs.

Press Releases

With a press release you can end up getting free advertising from National and local television, radio, newspapers, consumer magazines and trade publications. In fact the sky's the limit. The more media that you can expose your information to the better chance you have of actually getting something written about you. Try not to send out isolated press releases because if you've spent a long time working on your headline and content you need to make sure that you roll it out on a big scale to as many media companies as possible.

It's very easy to do and costs virtually nothing, apart from your time to write the release and the cost of the postage and it will bring in extra clients as you brand yourself as an authority.

Publicity in the media is far more powerful than any advertising that you can buy. In the eyes of the reader it gives you more credibility as you haven't paid to be there, and therefore will gain you instant trust. If you can get repeat exposure you'll gain expert status as people will say, wow that woman is in the papers every week, she must be good! People decide who the experts are, and by telling your story and by putting yourself forward has little to do with your actual ability in the hair and beauty industry. Whoever has the attention of the media wins.

Most of the press releases that journalists receive however end up going straight in the bin. Make sure yours isn't one of them. You need to think about the publication that you're targeting and what it offers to their readers, and then think about the journalist and what type of information they need to fill the huge amount of white space they have on their pages that will add value to their reader's lives.

It's worth noting here that journalists are not interested in you or your company history, they don't really want to know how long you've been established or about how amazing you are. They want a meaty story that will be interesting to their readers. So remember that if the headline of your press release goes something along these lines – Beauty Salon celebrates being in business for ten years – that is sure to find its way to the bin, but if the headline were to say – Beauty Business comes of age and to celebrate the staff are doing a bungee jump with their faces painted red, white and blue is by far a more creative headline and the journalist will surely read on.

The layout of your press release is very important. Start with a small date on the first line and then a large heading that has impact and compels the journalist to read on. Follow this with your press release and then finally a very brief description about you, your company and address. Finish with your contact information and website details. Try to keep your press release to just one A4 page. If you have to use two pages it will tell the journalist that you don't know how to get to the point quick enough and it'll put them off.

Remember that:

- Journalists need plenty of information for their readers, so make sure your press release is meeting those needs.
- Your press releases ideally should be controversial and solve a problem.
- Your press release should be a great source of information on the industry. Position yourself as an expert.
- Your press release can capitalise on recent news topics in the media so act immediately – even if it means writing it just before bedtime.

Think about how impressed your clients would be if they saw your competitor on television, and think about how that would make you feel!

I have a great little story to tell you about the power of press releases, and believe me, if you have not yet given it some thought on how you can get your business into the media, start now as the opportunity is out there for you.

A couple of years ago when the credit crunch had just started and things were full of doom and gloom in the media (not much difference from now) and the news was full of reports on business closures and the dreadful economic downturn, our local TV station did a report on the town where my shop and party venue was located. This report was extremely negative with the emphasis on the demise of the area and the untold quantity of empty shops. Our town was no different from most other towns in the country as the recession was hitting everywhere. I became angered about this TV report. How dare they criticize my town, how dare they say that all businesses there were in trouble and how dare they label the area as a ghost town. I immediately put pen to paper and sat down and wrote a press release stating that the information that had been broadcasted on television had not been the true facts. My retail shop and party venue (in the ghost town) was seeing fast growth in income and customer retention and in fact was making more money now than it ever had!

I sent a copy of this press release letter to the local newspapers, and waited for a response. I didn't have to wait long as the very next day the video crew arrived and filmed me at my Fairy School which I ran in my venue, followed by a further two newspaper interviews. When asked why my business was thriving whilst others around me were collapsing, I told them that it was due to my positive thinking and keeping in contact with existing customers. Within a week I was on the front page of one newspaper and page five of another with my video showing on the news websites. I also received a personal letter from the chief executive of the borough council, thanking me for such kind words about the town!!

It was so refreshing in the weeks that followed as so many people came in to the shop to congratulate me on doing so well in these 'awful times'!!!

I watched the local news and acted on an immediate opportunity to get myself into the newspapers and this is what you must also do. Start looking for opportunities around you, and this will become a massive power of branding as you become a public figure with specialist status. Listen intently at the stories on your local news programmes and ask yourself if there's a problem that you can solve. Maybe you have strong opinion on something topical or can look at an issue through the eyes of an expert. Read newspapers and national magazines, and listen to the gossip in the street and what your customers are saying. All these places could provide you with an ideal opportunity for your press release. All it takes is ONE of those opportunities to get you going. And when you see the impact that it can cause then you'll start doing it more and more. Look for opportunities wherever you can and turn negative situations into positive ones. Everyone loves a 'feel-good' story.

Presentations

Offer to do a presentation talk about your company at local networking groups. In fact anywhere that your target market hangs out – ask for a short time-slot of about ten-minutes to give a presentation, to hand out leaflets or to demonstrate your skill.

Awards

Another fantastic way to raise awareness of your business is to enter as many awards as you can. These can be on a local or national basis, to even an international basis. Keep a look out and even search the Internet to find the types of competitions you'd like to enter. Awards can also be nominated to you by your client recommendations. Not only will this massively boost your self-esteem but will also have a big impact in how you can sell yourself.

Alliances

Forming an alliance, or joint venture, with a complimentary company or an allied service provider is a great way for you both to capitalise on each other's customer lists. A sort of piggy-back relationship. This could be done through dedicated pages on each other's websites, or leaflets and promo banners. It may also be possible for you to piggy-back onto another businesses newsletter campaigns. Try giving away free gifts and coupons for each other's company, try doing a joint promotion (an overall 15% discount if the client books an appointment for both of your services) or you could even spend an afternoon in an allied salon to promote your services and give a percentage back to the salon for every client who books your service. The list can be quite endless when you put your mind to it.

If you have ten joint ventures or alliances and each one is only minimally productive with say only one new client coming in each month from each alliance that means that by the end of the year you will have had 120 new clients. Yes 120 new clients. That additional income will be a welcome surprise! Work on some alliances and joint ventures today. Who would you like to have in your gang? Who can help you, and who can you help? Compile a list and include the benefit and impact that they could have over your business.

Reciprocal Referrals and Recommendations

We all know that word of mouth is great for any business, but you need to go one step further in order for you to profit from it by implementing some sort of referral system. I love systems – you've probably realised that by now though! It's all very well that Mrs Jones has been singing your praises to Mrs Smith, but if Mrs Smith does no more than listen to her friend, and not act upon it and make an appointment with you, then quite honestly it's a total waste of a good conversation, and breath.

Don't wait for referrals to self-generate, you need to take the bull by the horns and make them happen by giving your clients a good and solid reason to do so. By planting the seed early on in your client relationship and by providing first-class service results your they will be only too pleased to pass your information onto their acquaintances who they feel could benefit from the same service that you have provided for them.

Refer and Reward systems are very easy to set up at any stage of your business life, and it goes without saying that the earlier the better. During your time spent with Mrs Jones you need to slip it into the conversation that you have a referral system in place whereby any client that refers will be rewarded. Ask Mrs Jones about her friends and family and whether she feels that any one of them could benefit from the same or similar service that you have provided. If she only gives you one name as a referral then that's a start in the right direction. Before you leave ask her to write the details of this contact down on your specially prepared referral card. Let her know that if her word-of-mouth generates a new client for you she'll be legible for a reward from you. This will encourage her even more so to tell her friends all about you and to help spread the good word. Give her a handful of your business cards and leaflets to help with this process.

Now it's most important here to make sure that all new clients who come to you are asked 'How did you hear about me'. They might say from a leaflet that they picked up in the library, by looking at your website, from a networking event or from Mrs Jones down the road. Straight away, there are two opportunities to be rewarded – the library and Mrs Jones.

You'll need to decide what shape and form the reward will be in and how much will it cost for you to implement it. The reward that you chose to give to your client can come in all shapes and sizes from discount vouchers and gift cards to a free manicure or eyebrow shape at their next visit. An even better type of referral reward to your client would be to send them something unexpected and not connected to your business in any way like a cinema ticket, a book voucher, a box of chocolates or simply a hand-written thank you card. This will do wonders for your business as your client will feel truly valued and will continue to recommend you to others, and each time she does, you reward with a different gift. It's a win-win situation.

Depending on the nature of the service supplied to your newly referred client will determine the expenditure you make on the gift to reward the client who referred. Pack the gift and post straight away to the referring client and don't forget to include a hand-written note (more personal) of your gratitude. This will do wonders for your business as your client will feel truly valued and will continue to recommend you to others, and each time she does, you reward with a different gift.

If Mrs Jones is good enough to refer a new client each and every week then the gift rewards must keep coming each and every week. Never miss or never forget. She'll be so impressed by your system and the fact that a little freebie arrives frequently that she'll continue to sing your praises on a regular basis and as loud as she possibly can. Again this is another win-win situation you can find yourself in!

As your business grows along with your client list you will find that by providing a good hair or beauty service will bring about recommendations to others from those who have been happy with the quality that you provide. Word of mouth is by far the best form of advertising that you could ever wish for. The words spoken by others about you hold more influence and will have much more impact than anything you could ever write in an advert or say about yourself.

~~~~~

CHAPTER 18

Advertising Online

Your Online Presence

Online marketing is by far one of the most profitable marketing strategies that there is for your hair or beauty business and it's without a doubt my most favourite form of marketing. This is a huge area to explore and when done properly it can be extremely profitable for you. Your online marketing should be put on consistent auto-pilot where possible and become systematic in defining what problems your clients are having so that you can solve them and put a marketing plan in place.

Website Creation

To be in business without a website is like being a window cleaner without a ladder. The two go together, hand-in-hand. Always have, always will. You should, however, have your *own* website, and not one of these free ones that have adverts and pop-ups, and not just space either on any of the chat forums like Facebook, MySpace and Bebo. You need your *very own creation*, your own shop window for your clients to look into.

In this day and age you will find that before a client does business with you, they will want to check you out first before contacting you by telephone or email to see what you're all about. Even if you come highly recommended – they will still like to get a visual feel for you before they strike. Gone are the days when a brochure or leaflet would suffice. People are hungry for a lot more information and they have a lot more choices out there – so make sure you're up there with the rest of your competition, or you won't get a look in. Your very own shop window will become a place for people to browse into at their leisure so your website should be properly dressed with the correct information and pricing so that it is a desirable place to be for your client in this Internet shopping mall.

Website marketing, when done properly can be extremely profitable as it's not that difficult to rank high in the search engines for your local area, or to track and analyse your site visitors in order to see just how many are converting to clients if you know how to do it effectively.

If you choose a web designer to create your website you need to make sure that there is a content management system in place, and you would need to know if there are any restrictions on the frequency of updating your site and of course how much this will cost you. Don't believe though that you have to have a professionally built website by a web designer in order to compete on the Internet. Another route to follow would be to design the website your-self using a software programme such as Dreamweaver or WordPress. This will give you greater control of how you manage your site with regards to updating the content (which incidentally should be done regularly in order to stay on top of the search engine rankings). You will also have more control over installation of your autoresponder, PayPal buttons and site statistic analyzers.

If producing your own website you'll spend a considerable amount of time in building and designing it and one of the most overlooked facts is how you're going to let people know that you're out there. When you move home do you send people that you know a postcard to inform them of your new address or do you just let them play the guessing game and hope that with trial and error of going down every close, avenue and road in the neighbourhood where they think you might be living they will eventually stumble across your new home by accident!! This is so very true for your website. You do the rough draft, you then design it, you then get it hosted, and you then wait for the business to come flooding in. But no one comes. No one knows you're out there.

A major way to get your site noticed is through your search engine optimization, SEO, which is something that you should commit to yourself as once you get the hang of it, it becomes second nature as you build your website. Don't be fooled by sales reps when they telephone you saying that they can guarantee you high rankings and page one on Google. This is totally untrue as no one can guarantee you space at the top. You must let the world and its brother know where you are through your title pages, your alt tags, your keywords and keyword-phrases, your hyperlinks, your inbound and outbound links and of course your offline advertising. Wow that's a long list isn't it – and the bottom line is, it has to be done if you want to be found. Avoid having a hush-hush website that no-one can find.

Before you go ahead and design your website you must know what its purpose is. Is it just a shop window, will you be selling from it, is it an information site, is it there to build relationships with potential clients? You'll probably find that your website will have one key element overall which is to convert visitors into buyers. Most visitors arriving at your website have done so because they chose to – so don't let them leave. Reinforce their time with you by giving them enticing and interesting items to read. You can accelerate your expert status with articles, reports, statistics, free gifts, competitions and any other information relevant to the industry. Your site must be full of exciting information that your visitor will find constructive as you only have eight seconds to make a first impression with them before they click through to another site and bounce right out. Not long, eh!! So make sure you are giving them what they have come for, immediately, or else they will just move on and they'll probably be gone forever.

If your visitors are arriving on your site via a landing page, from either search results, directory listings, social media links or domain strings then make sure that these pages give clear and simple instructions as to what the visitor needs to do. Remember direct response advertising – what do you want your visitor to do. Your landing pages don't need to be over flashy with mountains of copy. Keep them clean and keep them simple. Give the visitor limited choices in what they should do next or too many options will add to confusion and they'll leave your site in a clickety-click. If a landing page is also a sign up page for them to add their details for your newsletter only give them two options – either sign up or to go. This is known as a squeeze page. Give your client an incentive to take action now, make it clear and make it compelling for them to do so.

By having your contact details on every single page, if the client wishes to telephone you or to email you and they would like to do that now, they haven't got to go searching for your contact information. You could also put your telephone number under certain paragraphs throughout your site in a small font and in a lighter colour to the body text. Try it and see what happens. Test, test and then test again! It's always a good idea to have an About Us page which outlines a brief summary of who you are and this will make you become a real person.

When starting to build your site don't fall into the trap of running out of time or motivation to see your project through. Persevere. Blank pages on your website that are 'under construction' will send out a message that you're not on top of your game and will be just like having a naked mannequin in your shop window that people do a double-take to. Make sure all your content is complete before uploading it and think twice about putting a 'naked' page out there.

By designing your own site will benefit your cash flow in the long run as you will not need to keep paying your designer to update your site for you, and you will also be able to test and measure its performance easily, quickly and whenever you feel the need. So what are the fundamental elements that you should be testing on your site, and what results should you be recording?

1. Well number one is clearly your traffic. Test how many visitors are being attracted to your site and where they came from, and how did they find you. Did they come via a search engine or was it their keywords and key-phrases that they used? How many bounces do you get? A bounce incidentally is when visitors come into your site and very quickly go back out again.
2. Test the activity of the pages they are visiting once they are there, and how do they navigate your site?
3. Test your conversion rates on how many visitors you had to how many became actual paying clients.
4. Test different headlines and test different copy. If you do this regularly you will be able to pinpoint what works and what doesn't.
5. Test the offers and gifts that you are giving to your clients.
6. Test Pay Per Click advertising and Adwords.
7. Test article marketing by submitting to article directories.

Your website should be improved and updated on a regular basis – at least once a month, but weekly is more ideal. Test changing the front page from its usual layout. Change the headlines and tweak the body text. Change the colours, sizes and styles of your fonts. This process is ongoing and should never end or be put on the back burner.

You could have the best website in the world with finely crafted headlines, excellent content, fantastic photographic evidence and compelling call to actions which entice in a flood of visitors – but if you aren't keeping track of results and daily activities, then quite honestly you're not helping with your online presence.

I make it a regular discipline to track, measure and record all the following areas of my websites:

- How long the visitors stay on my site
- What pages they visit when they are there
- How they found me, search engine, direct link
- What location or country they are they from
- How they navigate my site
- What keyword searches they use

... and that's just for starters!

So perhaps now is the best time to install a website analyser in order to track the effectiveness of your site and its pages to give you a better understanding of what your potential clients are looking for, and what they are doing. You may find that you have a high bounce rate on one of your pages meaning that this page isn't working to its fullest potential, as it's not holding your visitors interest. You'll get a better understanding of all the pages on your site and will be able to plan for any improvements. Once you get going with your analyser you will gradually begin to understand the behaviour patterns of your visitors and what makes them convert into a buyer. By tweaking, changing and updating your sites content on a regular basis will not only help with your search engine rankings, but will also make for a better visiting experience for your visitor. Your website will become more influential in a way that you control and it will work hard for its keep and not just become yet another stagnant site out there in cyber-space!

Take a long hard look at your website (if you have one already) and do a checklist of all those key areas that you should be testing and recording results on, on a regular basis and after you've done that make sure that your site is as optimized as you can possibly make it and then submit it – with confidence - to the search engines. You've spent good money on your website or many hours of manual labour getting it ready and getting it out there, so don't leave it to chance and hope that your window shoppers are okay when they're spending time with you. Check it out and check it often!

Online Directories

Don't forget to take advantage of the many trade related directories that hold a presence on the internet. Simply search for these by placing a keyword followed by directory i.e. "beauty directory" (remember to use "quotes" to prevent having to trawl through a load of random searches) and add your company information to as many as possible of these. It will take a little time to do but believe me it's time well spent.

Some will allow you to add photographs and editorial copy, and some are even happy for you to provide a link back to your website. The majority of directories are free for you to add your details to and some may ask for a small annual fee for inclusion, either way they're a really good platform for you to use to get your message across to your potential client. Another great feature of directories is that it is a form of viral advertising as other directories will seek you out and add you unknowingly to their very own directory, and so the process goes on and on and you can end up being listed on many, many directories without having to do the legwork!

Social Networking

Social networking is a fabulous way to promote yourself and your business. By using Facebook, Twitter, LinkedIn, Instagram and Pinterest will give you a huge opportunity to sell yourself to your clients. It's on here that you can promote special offers, new products and service information and to place yourself as an expert in your field by sharing top tips and tricks of the trade.

If you decide to get a specific Facebook Page or Twitter account using your business name then go for it – blow your trumpet as loud as you can to engage your captive audience and on a daily basis post events, happenings, discounts, promotions, launches, elite packages, photos and as many top tips as you possibly can. If you have a blog that can automatically be fed through to your social media accounts then do that too.

Remember to put your fair share of usual posts that aren't just business related otherwise you'll be perceived as dull and only business focused. By doing this, sharing a few snippets of your personal life about your family and pets if you have them will make you become a 'real' person that your clients can relate to. Get the mix right and this can be a great arena to help grow your business. You'll need to keep your personal profile and business page separate though as you may not wish for your clients to be informed about any boozy nights out!!!

There are so many fantastic marketing strategies within social media to explore and implement, but way too many to write about in this chapter........so another book is in the making. To be notified of availability please email me at sherrill@mimicks.co.uk for details.

Email Marketing

Your existing clients can provide you with rapid growth to your business almost immediately. They have bought from you once before so they trust you as a service provider. You can continue to build a relationship with them over the coming weeks, months and years on the basis of your research into what they want, what are their unfilled needs and what strong desires they have at that moment. Email marketing has proven to be a real cutting-edge approach and you'll not believe the intensity of it until you've tested it and measured its response rate.

Email marketing shouldn't be used to just primarily sell your service as it should be used as a relationship-building tool. You can very easily adapt an effective email marketing campaign and decide on how often you are going to send out valuable information to those clients who have purchased from you before, which will in turn lead to further purchases of your services or products.

Your email campaign could be a monthly newsletter, or a special report on the hair and beauty industry that you can mail to your clients. If you have difficulty thinking of fresh content, start asking your clients what they would like to know about. Research that information for them and then inform them of it. Devise a product or service based on their answers and market to them straight away. Include tips and advice, take excerpts from your trade magazines and use them as articles (noting the author source). Contact an alliance of the industry and ask if they would like to place a small article within your newsletter. Hold competitions, everyone likes to have a go at winning something. The list can be endless when you put your mind to it.

Let them get to know you so that they understand that the information you have to offer them is of value and you're not just going for the hard sell. Send them advice, recommend a product and even send them to a link where they can receive a free gift voucher and this will go a long way to them having trust in what you do.

Great ideas for your newsletter could include:

- A write-up from an expert in the industry
- Articles taken from trade magazines
- A report on the latest 'hot' products or services
- Hair or beauty statistics you may read about in a newspaper
- Read a good book and write a review on it
- Watch a film at the cinema and write a review
- Try out a new product or piece of equipment that isn't related to your industry and write all about it
- Recommend another therapist/stylist and report on how brilliant they are
- Provide a recommended list of websites that you have visited that have great information that you'd like to share, not necessarily industry related
- Discuss your latest service that you are providing
- Discuss a product range that you're using and give a complete outline of its benefits to the consumer

There's so much information at your fingertips that you can use to benefit and enrich your clients lives with. The information that you send them will be welcomed and they'll look forward to seeing your name in their inbox.

Many restaurant owners use their email campaigns in a most successful manner to send free meal gift vouchers to customers just before their birthday. The offer is for a free meal for the birthday person and as no one generally dines alone on their birthday, there is a good chance that they will bring extra full paying friends with them. This is a win-win situation, the owner wins and the customer wins, and it also provides the restaurant owner with the opportunity to obtain some more email addresses along with birthday dates to put into the system and start the whole process again. WOW, what a fantastic system!! And for you as a service provider there are vast opportunities here for you to think about and unfold as well.

When emailing to your client database make sure that you put the full URL link to your website at the signature section in your newsletter as you'll want to entice them back onto your website. You could even try not writing the complete article or story in your newsletter and have a clickable link back to your website that says click here to read the rest of the story. In your signature section (sometimes called resource box or bio box) you could also write "Do you have a question – click here to email, which takes them straight through to a contact page on your website.

Now in order to have a great email campaign going you need to have a database of clients, but don't worry if you haven't started one yet as from now on in you must make it a requirement to capture as many email addresses as you can from your enquirers, your existing clients and through the visitors on your website. If you don't do this the opportunity could disappear for you to start building a relationship with these people and you're throwing away a golden opportunity to sell to them at some stage in the future. You must, must, must however have permission to add client email addresses to your database so you either need to ask for permission by explaining what your intentions are or the better method is to get them to fill in their information on a sign-up form that is situated in your website. This sign-up form is usually hosted by a third-party (a communication provider that supplies you with an autoresponder) and the client/visitor will need to confirm her details by opting-in to your newsletter. Another great thing about autoresponders is that your messages to your clients can be personalised with their name so when you hit the send button for your newsletter to be emailed out to your complete database, each one will land in their inbox with their own personal name on it. You'll be able to try out using different combinations such as Dear Sally, Hello Sally, Hi Sally or just Sally to see which ones work best for you.

Do be aware that the more information fields that you include in your sign-up form up may become a barrier to the visitor as they may not be happy to give too much information, so simply asking for their name and email address is usually more than enough. However if it is a simple and easy process you will unfortunately attract many people that are not necessarily your target market which you may not want. If you'd like to qualify your clients you can ask a series of additional questions other than just their name and email address and the sign up process takes longer to complete. This way you'll get a far better qualified person as they are more genuine. Always make sure that you offer something of value to your sign ups like a free report or discount voucher. Ideally sign-up boxes should be positioned at the top of your web pages to grab attention and never hidden away at the footer. Take a random look at six different websites that are not necessarily in the hair and beauty industry, and note what they ask for when completing their sign-up box and where their sign-up boxes are positioned on their websites.

Once you have your email campaign up and running you need to test it on a weekly, fortnightly or monthly scale, to see what works best for you and your client. Try to keep the style of you email consistent but don't be afraid of changing the content from a long one to a short one and from an information article to a sales article. You need to get the balance right here as you don't want to be bombarding your client with sales material all the time and only occasionally value-adding articles. They will too easily ask to be unsubscribed from your list if this is the case. So remember – more information based articles and a lot less of the sales pitch.

Remember to regularly test and track your email campaigns and if you have a good autoresponder there should be a report/analytics area where you can track:

- What time did the email arrive in their inbox
- How many emails were actually opened
- Did they forward it on to another person
- How many bounces did you have
- How many enquiries it generated

You should also track yourself as to:

- How many sales were made
- How many leads and referrals came in

Devise a one-year plan on how you're going to communicate with your clients. Plan out a rough draft of the email sequences that you're going to send and include topical articles and information that relates to specific times in the calendar such as Easter, Summer holidays, Halloween, Christmas Partytime, etc, etc. Ideally you need to plan your email marketing sequences well in advance and decide on how often you are going to send out to your database. Another great thing about autoresponders is that you can add all your newsletters into it at once and schedule in specific times for them to be sent out to your list.

Your email campaign is a communication device and a means of building relationships with your clients with you being the master of information that will add value to their lives. Keep them well informed with articles of interest and they will look forward to receiving them and not click away at the sight of your name in their inbox. Many of my customers say how much they look forward to my emails as it keeps them fully informed and up to date. Your emails need to be imaginative, diverse, captivating, appealing and humorous – totally unlike any others that they receive. This has been an extremely rewarding marketing tactic that I use in my primary business, and by putting into place an effective email marketing campaign I was able to increase my yearly turnover by 28%. All down to email marketing.

You too can gain immense profit by implementing some simple email marketing tactics into your business bringing in extra revenue that your clients would otherwise be spending elsewhere. Relationships with your clients can be your biggest asset if nurtured correctly.

The information I've supplied you here on online marketing is quite frankly a drop in the ocean as there is so much more out there for you to use in your hair and beauty business like I've done that will help you to attract high value returning and paying customers and clients to your website. But that of course is another book from me!

~~~~~

CHAPTER 19

Sales Process

Would You Buy Your Service?

If you were the client, would buying your product or service be the right choice to make or is there a better option available in the market place. Think long and hard about why your client should do business with you and not your competitor, what are you offering that they aren't? You must be able to answers these questions positively because if you can't it will mean that you haven't sold the idea or concept to you yet and that's a big problem to face. An important sale to make is selling you on you. Do you believe in yourself and what your business stands for? Do you have self-esteem in what you do? Are you confident and enthusiastic? How do you perceive your own self-image? If you shy away when enquiries are made from prospective clients then you need to re-visit your purpose for being in business. If you don't have confidence in what you do how on earth can you expect your clients to? You should also be able to make sure your clients are qualified to sell to as you can't sell vintage champagne from a market stall. You must decide that it's ok to sell to them and definitely don't waste time trying to sell to those who don't qualify because they're looking to bag a bargain. Are they suitable and are they going to purchase at the right price.

Are you following up on each enquiry that you get in your hair or beauty business with a solid sales system, or are you one of those business owners who receive a call from an interested person, deals with the enquiry and never do anymore than that? This is where you can excel with an outstanding sales process behind you.

When a client has responded to an advert of yours, whether it's a paper-based advert or from a poster placed out in the local community or from a leaflet given out – have you got in place an efficient sales process? Think about it now – what does *your* sales process entail?

An exceptional sales process could go along these lines:

- Advert placed in a publication or leaflet handed out.
- A new client telephones to enquire about what you can offer them.
- You discuss their requirements in detail and offer advice. They may book an appointment in this first point of contact, if not:
- You ask for their email address or direct them to your website where they'll see your sign-up form. They may then book you, if not:

- You send them some information, reports, incentives - all value adding. They may then book you, if not:
- You continue to build a relationship with newsletters
- Over time, and after they've gotten to know you they could eventually make an appointment for one of your services. You've built the know, like, trust factor.

This is just a generalized process. In order to surpass what you already do you would need to list each and every step of your process and improve on each and every element. You need to think to yourself – how can I make this better for the client, how can I add more value for them, how can I improve on my client care. Small improvements that you make can be the page of the website that you direct them to, the words that you use when you first speak with them to the free special report that you send out to them. If you make small incremental changes to each element in the way that you do business with your client, you'll possibly see changes in peoples buying decisions as they happen.

All of your contact steps should be recorded and monitored to enable you to see your actual conversion rate and at what stage of the process it's likely to take place. By doing this you will have a better understanding of your sales process and what it will take to convert to a sale.

Its wise noting here again like I've done in a previous chapter that peoples' buying decisions differ vastly and it could take a number of contacts between you and the prospective client to secure an appointment. Your client will indeed go on a journey to buy from you rather than making an instant decision. The words "No not now" or "No not today" can eventually make you money. No is not forever, as No just means not this moment in time. We all say no and then change our mind due to our circumstances. Become positive about no not today as it means that the client will just be put back into your sales process and you can start it all over again with them. People these days lead extremely hectic lives and most of the time they have an awful lot going on. Booking an appointment for your service today may not be their number one priority as they have a great deal to get done, but in time priorities and state of affairs change and they may well come back to you, as long as you have given them something of value to remember you by. You need continuous ongoing contact as the client might not buy today, tomorrow or even next month, but with continuous contact they could buy in the future.

Think of how you make decisions on buying something. When you buy a new piece of furniture do you buy the first dining table that you see? Of course you don't, so you enter into a buying process, which will be something like this:

1. Decide you need a new dining suite
2. Look in some magazines and/or surf the web
3. Think about the price you can afford
4. Go to a showroom, speak to a sales person and take away a brochure
5. Look at the brochure and price compare on the Internet
6. Go back to the showroom
7. Make a decision
8. Buy the furniture or start the whole process again

If the above scenario was for a client seeking say a new hair style then you would come into their lives at point 4. They decide they need a new look, they surf the Web, they think about their budget, they contact you. Don't forget that they've already gone through steps 1-3 and at number 4 you will be right there with your competitors, so it's at this point you must be ready to make a good impression. This is where you become a mountain of knowledge and answer all their questions, meet their needs, explain the benefits of what they have chosen and guide them gently through the whole buying decision process. And then this is where you need to capture the details of your client in order to put them into your sales process.

Most one-stop selling doesn't work, i.e. one point of contact, one phone call, one visit to your website. You need to have a multi step marketing system with your prospective clients as their buying patterns are like a rotating cog-wheel – each click will move them closer to the sale. Whether its six steps or twenty-six steps, follow up with a set process to your enquiries. You have an absolutely perfect reason to keep in contact with people who make enquiries with you.

Make a list of your usual multi-step sales process (it may however be only two steps at the moment) and decide on small changes to improve on each element. Next add some new steps to your process to really push for the maximum exposure and then as before continue to change and improve. Also include the following information:

- The scripts you will say on the phone and your leading questions.
- The information you will send out to them for free, to add value.

- The information you will gather on them to use at a later date.
- The timings and procedures of your follow-ups.

Devise some sort of table that you can use as a checklist and diary for incoming enquiries and to record your actions. Review your sales process on a regular basis so that it never becomes stale.

Important steps to take when selling to clients and how to influence them is to allow them to ask the questions, as many as possible. You can also prompt for information by asking open-ended questions that will encourage them to speak and you'll be able to get a good understanding of what it is they're wanting. Don't start telling people about what you do and how great you are and how fantastic your service is until you have answered all their questions and have found out what's important to them. Then hand-pick from your services what you perceive is of being the greatest value to that client. Incidentally, take this to the extreme whereby you don't blow your own trumpet about how good you are – it's all about keeping the balance right with regards to letting them talk to find out what they want and then letting them know that you're able to fill all those needs by telling them what you can do for them.

When dealing with person to person (and not over the phone) use good body language. Breathe at the same rate as them and speak with the same volume and tone and this will certainly bring a sense of rapport between you (it works and it's quite a fun thing to do)! Look relaxed and open to questions. Nod your head in the right places and be genuinely interested in what your client is saying. They will immediately pick up on it if you look even slightly disinterested or are unsure on how to answer certain questions. If you have people working for you make sure they are aware of this too. Try testing a few body language postures on a friend or family member and you'll find that it is really easy to do and it's so very effective. Google up body language to get some ideas of what you can do to promote effective communication.

You will of course come across objections - objections to price, objections to perceived value and objections to your product or service - and when you hear them you need to be ready with your answers. Make sure that you continually ask questions and really, really listen to what the client is saying. Don't beat-about-the-bush. Tell them how it is. This is always a good time to pull out some testimonials from satisfied clients, which will reinforce what you're offering them. If they say that they can't afford it, you then know that their objection is to price so you can then re-establish the value that it will make to them. Keep a running list of the objections that you get and write down the answers to these objections as a sort of script which will become a great resource for you. You may be lucky and they purchase from you in this first instance, but hey, if not don't worry about it as they may indeed become a client in the near future. Continue to build a relationship with them with low-pressure communication.

Don't Be a Pushy Sales Person

I expect you've had a conversation with a sales rep at some time or another, who has telephoned you to try to sell you something. You can sense that there is no passion, no enthusiasm, and no real interest in you by the tone of their voice. They just want to sell you something so that they can make some money in commission, which you can sense instantly. On the other hand how would you feel if that sales person went the extra mile and did whatever it took to make *your* life easier, to understand and solve *your* problems, to add value to *your* life, to decipher *your* troubles and meet *your* requirements – wouldn't you just love it!

So many of us switch off when that impending sales phone call comes through. We're just not interested. And why aren't we interested? Because it's the same old thing – pushy sales person blabbering on about how magnificent their service or product is and how much we need it. How does he or she know whether we need it or not? Have they asked any questions to find this out? Probably not. So what do we do – well we switch off and try to tell the sales person about four or five times that we're just not interested. They then become all defensive and ask why we're not interested and they then take it as a personal insult! Eventually you'll put the phone down and mutter to yourself on how rude that pushy sales person was. If you can even begin to remember what company they were representing, that indeed will make you feel a negative pre-disposition towards it. Think about a recent telephone call that you have gotten from a sales rep recently. Before you read on, take a minute or two to think about all the aspects that you disliked about these high-profiled sales calls.

Were your answers

- The sales rep was reading from a script, sounding like a robot and making you feel just like a random telephone number.
- The sales reps opening line was that it was just a courtesy call. Rubbish. It's wasn't a courtesy call it was a sales push.

- The sales rep was being really pushy and not taking no for an answer, and even worse when they questioned you on why you were saying no to them (as if it's any of their business).
- The sales rep was making false claims and lying to you. There is no such thing as a free cruise, a free timeshare and a free £5000.
- The sales rep puts the phone down on you without even saying thank you for your time and goodbye. How rude!

Now think about all the things that you like and admire when a decent sales rep calls, such as:

- The call was significant to you. They made a point to inform you that there is something in it for you. It has value.
- They asked you questions and they actually listened to your answers and then answered and reacted accordingly.
- They let you speak and they never butted in over the top of your words.
- They came straight to the point and didn't beat about the bush with fluffy sales talk.

In your hair or beauty business you don't want to be that pushy sales person, you don't want to intimidate potential client into purchasing and you certainly don't want to get a bad reputation for being too sales-y. You do, however, want to be conceived as understanding your clients needs, wants and desires, and you do want your reputation to soar due to the value that you are able to provide.

Next time you get one of those very annoying phone calls from a pushy sales person, as soon as it's finished make notes on all the aspects of the conversation that displeased you, that were irritating to you and that were just generally unprofessional. Look at your notes and think about how you could have scripted the conversation better. Maybe there were beneficial opportunities that the sales rep totally missed that could have helped with their selling process to you. Use this as a learning curve for your business and avoid making the same mistakes as they did.

Clients Love a Guarantee

Whether it's in your sales process, on your website or on a sales letter that you send out - clients love safety-nets, especially in today's economy. I'm sure you understand that, and also that it's totally acceptable from the clients point of view that they should have one too. So with this in mind you should be offering them a no-brainer, guarantee.

By adding a guarantee you will have put a full risk reversal in place for the client. A lot of big high street stores like M&S do this and they do it very well. It's their trusted business module. Customers have no risk when they buy from them with their money back guarantee that they have in place.

Have a solid guarantee in place for people who book any of your services and give them risk reversal as you should cover the risk and not them. It's the right thing to do and this will give you strength to sell well, providing you with weight. We used this strategy in our children's party venue and in our face painting business - if at the half way stage of their party they are not completely satisfied with our service we would give them a full refund, yes a full refund. Hand on heart – we have never gave out any refunds because no-one ever asked for one. So go on - try this out for your business.

~~~~~~

CHAPTER 20

Keeping Clients Informed

Don't Leave Clients in The Dark

By keeping clients informed in any areas that you feel may be of interest to them, and in line with your own business style, will most certainly create an expert status about you, and their confidence in you will grow as you position yourself as a trustworthy expert in the hair and beauty industry.

Maybe you read an industry trade magazine, if so you'll find that these publications are a fantastic source of information for you to use and to pass onto your clients. Filled with articles and photographs on the latest this and that and the hottest products on the market can all be used to keep your clients up-to-date and in the know.

However articles of interest, and snippets of information that you pass on to your clients don't necessarily need to be all about what you already do, or all about what you already sell. Quite the opposite in fact, as to share information with another that clearly has no immediate benefit to you will only serve to enhance your reputation. So keep a look out for articles of interest from other allied service providers as well.

A short email or text to your client could read along the lines of:

'Hey (name), I've just been reading my hair magazine and a fantastic new curly hair conditioner has just been launched. Thought of you immediately as it could be the dream product you've been looking for'.

Or how about 'Hi (name), recently you asked about a night cream – well XYZ has just had a fabulous review in my magazine about their latest skin care range which you can purchase on the High Street. This could be just what you're looking for'.

The above examples can be sent out to a specific target group or to a specific person – to all those clients with very curly hair or to an individual client who has discussed skin care products with you. Treat the way you send this information out as if you were chatting to a best friend and keep a conversation tone going with your emails and texts rather than trying to send out a formal editorial piece which could be off-putting. The above examples can be sent out to a specific target group or to a specific person. It's also possible to send out a generic message or email to your complete database, especially through your Facebook page and this could be worded as follows:

'Just seen an advert for a competition on the XYZ website to win a luxury day at a National Spa. It's a fantastic offer and the entry for the competition is a cinch. We could all do with some additional pampering to soothe our hectic lives don't you agree'. Then include the link to the competition or article.

Now the type of message above that you send out may not have any immediate benefit to you whatsoever, but there is a benefit to be had. It could quite simply serve as a memory jogger to a client who has been meaning to give you a call to book an appointment with you but hasn't quite got round to doing it. Your email is there sitting in her inbox and it will be so very easy for her to reply to you and say "Oh thanks for that, glad you contacted me because I've been meaning to phone you to book in for an eyelash tint". Another win-win situation!

These articles of interest that you pass on to your clients don't necessarily need to be all about what you already do, or all about what you already sell. Quite the opposite in fact, as to share information with another that clearly has no immediate benefit to you will only serve to enhance your reputation. So next time you're flicking through a magazine don't just look at products and services of interest to you, think outside the box and look for adverts and articles that could be of interest to your clients in a way that you can help to solve a problem of theirs, and the benefit to you will draw that much closer.

Adding to Your Repertoire

Most wealth in business comes from copying other successful businesses already out there in the market place. It's so much more difficult to think of absolutely brand new ideas and you certainly don't want to re-invent the wheel. That's why I'm such an advocate of reading influential business books in order to learn from others, networking at business seminars and attending courses and plenty of webinars.

Maybe now you're in a position where you're comfortable and confident with the services that you already provide to your clients, regardless as to whether that is a small select range or a substantial diverse assortment, and eventually there will come a time when you will want to reach out to add other services to your repertoire.

To get the very best chance of business growth, and for your business to succeed, it's so important to keep up-to-date with current trends as they materialize as our industry moves very, very fast. By offering your client an up to date product will ensure that you stay in the forefront of your field and this in turn will accelerate your reputation. Clients just love to be on the receiving end of something new, something innovative and something extraordinary so that they can brag about it at the school gates amongst their friends. Gaining knowledge and experience in any additional skill-set or product line is the essential key to growth. You'll never know everything there is to know about the services that you provide or the products that you use, it's impossible, because time doesn't stand still and every day new ways of doing things are being introduced and new and improved products lines are coming on to the market.

The very best beauty therapists, hair stylists, make-up artists and nail technicians in the industry, in the World in fact, still strive to improve their skills; they still attend training in specialised areas and make every effort to become familiar with the benefits of latest and up-to-the-minute products to hit the market. Even if you only choose to attend a one-day training course to advance your capabilities, you'll find that you will be completely re-energised within your business and you'll be inspired to add your newly acquired skill to your range as soon as you can. It's also never too late to once again return to college to gain further qualifications in other areas of the hair or beauty industry that you can offer as an additional and complementary service.

Complacency can be a very easy trap to fall into, and if you're not careful one day you may wake up to smell the coffee and realise that the World has moved on and not waited for you. Services, products and equipment can become out-dated as the new, the improved and the more beneficial emerge, and if your competitors are always one step ahead of you that could be the end of your business. So jump on the gravy train and keep on learning, and then after that learn some more!

Bringing New Services on Board

How often do you have one of those moments, when an 'Ah Ha' thought pops into your mind? You may become excited about the prospect of a new service to provide, or a new promotion that you can offer or a new product to sell. You put a lot of effort into the thought process behind this idea, analysing the significant profitable outcome – but in fact you may spend little or no time in actually putting it into practice and getting the thing going, only to despair when someone else does before you!

This is a case of analysis paralysis again.

Spending too much time in the thought process, mulling this and that over, time and time again, can lead to the new idea never even getting off the ground. Now I'm not saying here to just jump straight in with every conceivable idea you may have as that would just be too erratic, instead you should plan out a strategy for the launch of any new concept.

Your launch strategy could go something like this:

- Light Bulb Moment – make notes on paper to capture the thought before it's gone forever
- Research the idea, the product, or the service to get as much information as necessary to take it forward
- Check out its viability – is it something that your prospective client needs, wants or desires
- What is the end result that the client will experience and the benefit to them?
- Will it be conceived as a fad, a passing phase, or will it be here to stay?
- Work out the pricing strategy of how much it will cost to put it in place, how much you can sell it for and what are the profit margins?
- Decide on the best marketing angle to get it off the ground quickly
- Then JDFI, before anyone else does!

You don't have to spend countless hours on each of the above points as just a general overview will suffice. As long as you have all the important information covered you can take your idea forward as soon as you feel confident enough to do so. There is no time like the present and unfortunately time stands still for no-one. Get your new service, promotion or product out there as quick as you can and then you can move onto the next one. Don't become a victim to that analysis paralysis, which put another way means 'all talk and no action'. I expect you've come across a lot of people like that – those are the ones who say to you "Yeah, well I was going to do that but just didn't get round to doing it".

As the old saying goes "There are those that do, there are those that don't and there are those that watch others do".

Up Selling Isn't Rocket Science

How often have you placed an order with a company over the telephone and they have offered you an 'up-sell' – quite often I would expect. You know the kind I mean – you buy a wall clock and they ask if you'd like batteries, you purchase a burger and they say 'fries with that' or you fork out for a new television and they ask if you'd like to purchase an extended warranty. This is up-selling, a very effective marketing strategy.

You need to be in a position where you can do the same for your client as there is always a great deal of additional income to make from this great little marketing approach. Your up-sell can simply be an additional mini bonus service to add to the main service they are purchasing. You may choose to do a special offer limited for this month only, or a product or service that will compliment what they are buying or increasing the opportunity to pay for say a facial and offering a free eyebrow shape (a bit like bumping up from a regular size milkshake to a jumbo size milkshake). There are so many different opportunities of up-sells to be had; you just need to be creative in your thinking and decide what it is that you can present to your client. When I had my fairytale party venue, up-selling was offered to every single customer as normal practice that made a booking with us and more often than not they would purchase additional items such as balloons, party bags and birthday cakes. We even up-sold our regular Princess Party Hostess to Cinderella, Belle and Snow White. I would hazard a guess here and say that at least 85% of our customers purchased an up-sell of some sort to add onto their party. If my staff hadn't been trained to offer these up-sells at the time to the customer making the party booking, they would have purchased most of those items somewhere else and I would have lost the additional income to another shop.

Something else not to neglect is cross selling, which means to sell something that has an opposite connection to the product or service that they are buying. An example would be to book in a hair appointment and to also sell them French manicure nail polish products.

You could even produce an up-selling and cross-selling matrix that can be shown on your website where clients can choose their up-sell or cross-sell package to suit their requirements and needs. Package what you offer and give choices on rates as not all clients will be looking for the same outcome, so tailor to a variety of needs to maximize the best possible offers that you can. By offering and promoting up-sells and cross-sells will produce more sales to improve your cash flow and the added bonus is it doesn't cost anything more in advertising as there is no need to invest in new clients to do it – you promote it to the clients you've already got. Put in up-sells and cross-sells wherever and whenever you can for another win-win situation.

Special Promotions and Incentives

People just love to bag a bargain, especially the elite kind. So how about offering your client something that is that little bit extra special, or has money off for a set period or even to launch a brand new and exciting service. You'll find that your clients will be most responsive to give you a call to make an appointment.

There are so many different ways that you can offer a special promotion when you think about it. Why not offer them something special for their birthday, for Christmas or prior to their summer holiday. You could giveaway five specific new treatments in exchange for valuable client testimonials or maybe devise a membership package that could include exclusive member benefits with elite premium services or products that clients rarely purchase for themselves.

These types of marketing activities will be adding money to your bank and by taking the time to put some great elite a packages into place will support your business success.

Creating a Fan Club

It's one thing getting new clients and a completely different thing in keeping them. It takes time, effort and money in order to get each and every one of your clients and if you don't have some sort of system in place for making them stay loyal to you they'll be here today and gone tomorrow.

Systems for client retention will need to be put in place so that you can consistently monitor the effects that the impact of their profits can have on your business bank account. If you solely rely on a handful of clients to see you through and something changes in unforeseen circumstances to withdraw them from using you as their service provider, what impact will that have on you and your standard of living. Such circumstances could be anything from a new beauty therapist targeting your market, your nearest competitor drastically reducing their prices or the cost of your overheads increasing forcing you to put your prices up. As well as building a client database you also need to be building a 'fan' database. This is for the type of client that is very loyal to you and your company. I have a very large business to business 'fan' base that has been built over a considerably long time, and some of my corporate bookers have been loyal to my company for over two decades. Now that's a fan club.

So how do you get clients to become part of your raving fan base? Easy, you make them feel really, really special by doing certain things for a select few of them and treat them like royalty. Before you can start to build your fan base you need to take a long hard look at your client database in the first instance and ask yourself the following questions of each and every one of them:

- Do I have a good rapport with them?
- Have we built up a good level of trust between us?
- Have they been consistent with their run of appointments so far?
- Are they willing to try out my new services when launched?
- Do they have a good account history with me?

When looking at each individual client on your list, if you can honestly answer yes to each of the above questions – then without a doubt they need to be targeted for your raving fan base. So with your raving fan base built, which might incidentally be only about 20% of your overall client list, it's now time to put some marketing strategies in place for them.

Start by informing them that as a loyal client you are setting up an 'elite' club for a few of your best clients to be part of and that they have been invited to join (for no charge of course). People like things that are elite as it makes them feel special to be part of something that not everyone can get their hands on, whether that's a bottle of wine, a cocktail dress or a membership to a sailing club. Next have some sort of brochure printed that will outline the benefits to your fan base – making sure that they are all benefits or it will be a pointless exercise.

The benefits could include discounts on all future services that they book with you, price reductions on any of your retail product ranges, information on your new services planned well before your general clients get heed of them, a complimentary pub lunch voucher for two people on their birthday or a Christmas pamper hamper, or even a yearly outing with other fans, free of charge to a spa/dinner/theatre. The list above is just a starter and is not exhaustive as you can be as generous as you see fit to lavish your raving fans with whatever you so desire, within reason. Remember that this special little elite club is all about making them feel truly valued as a client of yours and that they are indeed being rewarded for their loyalty to you.

Just remember the reciprocation rule here – the more you give the more you'll get in return. I'm a strong believer in what goes around, comes around.

~~~~~

CHAPTER 21

Positive Thinking

Is Your Glass Half Full or Half Empty?

Positive thinking is a really significant aspect for your business success. You need to have a great attitude and mind set all the time which will help you through the hard times and how you deal with things is what will make all the difference. Your positive attitude will rub off onto your clients as will equally a bad attitude. There indeed will be times when your glass is half empty, and it's on those not so good occasions that you must flip the balance by looking on the bright side, find the good elements of the situation and strive for a more positive outlook.

You can turn other business peoples' behaviour patterns into a beneficial and positive format for the success of your own business. Think about those who have arrived at the place in the business world or in the hair and beauty industry where you want to be and get your behaviour patterns to match with theirs and a most important change will happen to speed your business progress up to the next level. You should model yourself on other people's successes. Literally choose any person in business, any business that inspires you no matter how big or small, that gives you motivation and that you would love to replicate. Make a study on them by gaining as much information as possible by looking at their website, their sales literature and speaking with their clients or customers if you can. Don't try to re-write their formula and re-invent the wheel because if it works for them then make it work for you. Become a magpie and feather your own nest with little bits and bobs from others that have inspired you.

To help you to get into a positive mindset every morning pick up a success related book and read it for about 5 minutes. That's all – just 5 minutes. You could even do this before you actually get out of bed. Soak up any positive ideas that you could implement into your business life and these ideas will be embedded into your sub-conscious. You'll be uplifted from the start of the day and you'll start to develop habits similar to those who you read about. Read as much as you can on a daily basis and fill your mind with vital material to sift and sort through. You can experiment with this by reading different and various view-points, diverse success biographies, business books and marketing publications. How many times have your read through a trade magazine and thought to yourself "I could do that". Business books and biographies will also instil the same positive attitude for you. Become inspired on a regular basis.

When you read a good book that inspires you, as you read through highlight all the points of interest and all the things you want to remember. After you've read the book go back over all the highlighted points and write them down on paper adding your own ideas and thoughts. Next type it all out and this will further embed it into your memory and reinforce your learning by three-times. Once on the first reading, secondly going back and hand-writing out all your highlighted points and thirdly by typing it out into a word-processor. Reinforce, reinforce, reinforce. It's a fantastic way of remembering things and something that I do quite often. If you have a selection of business books, celebrity biographies and trade magazines make a list of all the titles. Next to each title on your list write a brief sentence of what elements in the book or magazine you could use as a pick-me-up, something to inspire you. For instance a trade magazine will get your creative juices flowing, a business book will give you a positive mindset and a biography will motivate you to become great at what you do.

Hopes and Dreams

We all have hopes and dreams, maybe for a better life or a person we aspire to be. Maybe we want to be healthier, fitter, wealthier or more loved. You have to have hopes and dreams as this will give you something tangible to work towards. Build a portfolio of your desires and call it 'I want it, I deserve it and I will get it'. Positive thinking followed by positive documentation then positive actions leads to positive outcomes.

There will be occasions when you will be up to your neck in the stresses and the strains of organising and running your business and negativity may creep it. Don't worry – it happens to all of us. This is the time you should sit back, clear your mind and re-evaluate the reasons why you are in business and concentrate on thoughts that are positive and productive. This is so important as time to time you will have challenges and obstacles to overcome.

Get yourself into a better mood, pick up that inspiring book and synchronise yourself positively with your business – mentally, emotionally and behaviourally.

- Mentally – feed your mind with positive thoughts by reading articles and publications that will inspire you.
- Emotionally - book onto the next hair and beauty trade show where you can rub shoulders with like-minded individuals and become totally stimulated.
- Behaviourally – do something positive like create a new make-up design, hair style or piece of nail art.

Don't let any outside causes determine your business success for you as negative influences can paralyse you with fear. Whatever effect is about to happen or is happening it will be all too easy for you to blame your upbringing, where you live, the government, the media, or the economy for a failing business. Rise above any negativity that meets you face to face whether that is economic coverage in the news, friends voicing their negative opinions about your self-employment and family members trying to be of help but who are all too often putting doubt in your mind that you'll ever make a success in your business.

Maybe you have negative influences that are affecting you at the moment, whether personal like a friend pooh-poohing your business venture, or a business related issue like a new beauty therapist targeting your market? Implement positive ways in which to run your business and stop worrying and listening to others who harp on about negative influences and all too easily are ready to place blame on others. All of these negativities can infuse a fear of failure before you even get off the ground if you let them. You need to change your mind set and become optimistic, positive and forward thinking in everything you to on a daily basis. Shift gear into a more positive outlook and then look in the mirror and say out loud what it is you want to achieve, and say it often. As you sharpen your positive attitude you'll not only find that you'll rise above all the negative influences and possible criticism but you will leave all those non-believers standing there with their mouths wide-open!

You can also plan to make any negative situations that may arise into positive ones. Think seriously about what would happen if certain situations crept into your business life that you had little or no control over. What would happen if you lost your appointments diary, what would happen if you had a flood or fire at home, what would happen if your key staff member left if you had one, what would happen if you had a cash flow crisis, what would happen if you broke your wrist and couldn't work, your website crashes, your telephone is cut off, your partner walks out, someone steals your car with all your kit and equipment in it, or recession hits you really badly. WOW – that's a big list of negative situations.

You need to put contingency action plans and policies into place, and you need to put them into place now. Don't ever say "Oh that won't happen to me", or "That's not important for me to do yet" because the unexpected has a way of creeping up to bite us on the bum when we least expect it. So be warned – backup your computer documents today!! I think I better repeat that – back up your computer documents today.

Get Positive Today

So on the positive side and with your positive attitude you also need strong belief, confidence, desire, willpower, commitment and enthusiasm. Enthusiasm comes from the heart and it's very infectious. You're the only one that can make things happen in your business. Quite often I hear my customers say to me 'You're always so happy, you've got such a positive outlook'. Absolutely. There's no reason at all that you can't inspire the people that you come into contact with on a daily basis. Your positive thoughts will lead to strategy building, which in turn leads to implementation which leads to speed which builds momentum which leads to magnetism which leads to wealth in your business.

So here's a formula for success which you should write out in large words on a piece of card and stick it where you'll see it every day (by your computer, by your bed, in the downstairs loo, wherever):

→ **Positive Thinking:**
Look for positive opportunities
→ **Positive Opportunities:**
Build your future plans
→ **Implementation:**
Putting those plans into action
→ **Building Momentum:**
The habit will gather speed
→ **Magnetism:**
Speed attracts good things to you
→ **Wealth in Your Business:**
Goal

Get positive today and everyday – it's highly infectious.

~~~~~

CHAPTER 22

Your Golden Opportunities

Looking For Those Lucky Breaks

You may be in the initial start-up stage of your business or have been going for a number of months or years but I'm sure that you'll more or less be of the same mindset as me that running a business is all about keeping up with current trends, products and services and being in a position to act on those ideas for expansion as soon as they come to light. With the vast amount of information that is ready for us to grab and capitalise on, can sometimes make it difficult to spot an opportunity that can in fact be sitting right under our noses.

As your hair or beauty business grows look for opportunities wherever and whenever you can. You need to keep an open mind and not have tunnel vision just to suit yourself. Look, listen and learn and by doing this you'll open up a whole area of opportunities just waiting to be acted upon. Golden opportunities are everywhere around you and not only can they present themselves when you are having a conversation with a client, you should also be on the lookout for ideas from unusual sources.

Here are a few opportunity spotters to think about:

- Read a random magazine that you haven't read before as you'll never know what you'll come across that could be turned into a golden opportunity
- Travel to an appointment via an unusual route to see the neighbourhood or surrounding areas from a different perspective. You might see an advertising bill-board that gets you thinking about a new marketing angle
- Strike up a conversation with someone that you normally wouldn't pass the time of day with, like a taxi driver, the little old lady waiting at the bus stop or the sales assistant in the bakery
- Listen to a different radio station than normal, especially a talk show one
- Watch a different news channel
- Watch a couple of hours of breakfast television occasionally and see what pops up
- Join a network group of like-minded people and rub shoulders with as many people as you can there from a completely diverse range of companies

At the beginning of each working day, read the above list and as you go through the day you'll gradually start to focus on opportunities as and when they arise. By doing this and opening yourself up to situations that are different from the norm, you'll be extending your creative mind and somewhere along the line you'll say, "Ah, now that's a good idea, maybe I could do that too". Be open minded with everything and everyone and something good is sure to materialise!

You could also start with taking a long hard look at your business and where it stands now. Think about areas that are available to you which will add value to your clients lives by starting with your existing product or service:

- Can you improve your existing product or service?
- Can you enhance your systems in any way?
- Can you obtain a grant or an award?
- Can you make better arrangements with your suppliers?
- Can you speed up your clients booking in process?
- Can you obtain new contact sources?
- Can you devise original and enhanced ways of doing absolutely everything in your business?
- Is there anything in your industry that is old fashioned and obsolete? Can you update it?
- Can you devise a back-end product to a service that you provide either at a discounted price or as a free give-away?

- Can you improve your existing service by keeping it at the same price but having the benefits of being advanced or to the standard of a deluxe version?

Get your clients talking. Lead them into conversation but most importantly, listen to what they have to say. See if you can spot how they make their buying decisions and in what conditions. Casual conversations can in fact harvest something useful that you may have never discovered. Take a little test at the end of each week to help you re-focus and you may very well spot something that has been there all along:

- Who has spoken and presented me with an opportunity today?
- What are my clients telling me, what are they saying that they want and need?
- What is there an increased need for at this moment in time?
- What service or product would my clients buy today if I could offer it to them?
- What is different about my business / my clients / my industry / my competitor this week or month?

Every business owner needs thinking time. Day-dreaming as it can be known. I need thinking time to effectively move my business forward. Planning, organising in my head, system building in my mind.

No matter how busy you are in the day to day running of your hair or beauty business you should always make the time for your very own 'thinking time'. We all need thinking time in order to move our business forward. Your thinking time ideally should be done in a quiet place and preferably not in front of the television or with any other distraction to stifle your imaginative impulses.

Creating ideas and thinking about golden opportunities and building on them is fairly easy and most of us are capable of doing that, when we are in one of those daydreaming modes. The difficulty comes in putting those ideas into practice, seeing the challenges that each idea will possess and working out the path around the idea and its obstacles to its fruition.

Your inspirational ideas will often come to you when you're not at work, when you're relaxing and sometimes from the most unusual situations. This is because you are in a different mindset, away from the working environment and you're looking at things through a different perspective. My inspiration moments come when I am in bed at night, when I'm reading a book and when I'm walking my dogs. This is a relaxing time for me and my mind seems to work ten to the dozen and new ideas just keep popping into my head. Sometimes the ideas come so fast that I trip over them, and feel disappointed if I haven't got a pen and pad to hand to write them down. I now keep a notepad on my bedside table and will reach over and scribble things down so I don't forget them. If I don't, you can bet your bottom dollar that when I awake I can't for the life of me remember the remarkable script for a sales letter that I concocted to myself before nodding off!!

So with all the hustle and bustle that takes place when you're running your business it's important to find a little bit of thinking time at your very own inspiration location, where you can be on your own for a short while each day. This is a valuable time to revisit and contemplate any golden opportunities that clients may have presented to you through conversation along with any exciting ideas that you may have swimming around in your head which will help to move your business forward. Time allocated needn't be long for this process, as at least fifteen minutes daily will be enough for you to jot down notes as memory joggers that can be expanded on at a later date after you have added them to your 'to do' lists.

I've had many missed opportunities over the years and unfortunately I only have myself to blame for not being quicker off the mark! You may have once said, or heard someone say "Yeah well I was gonna do that". It's the classic case of someone beating you to your idea. If you don't write down your thoughts, ideas, hunches and instincts as soon as you can, they may be lost forever – that is until the time that your competitor has the same ones as you had and you turn a nasty shade of green!

Take action in your ideas, tasks, projects and key areas today. Don't hesitate and put off until tomorrow. Never use the "Oh I'm just too busy to do that" Time is the foundation on how everything works as timing is the difference between salad and garbage (probably my most favourite quote)!

Golden Opportunities are everywhere. What are your clients needs? What do they want? How can you give it to them and add massive value to their lives?

Think about it.

The **next chapter** you are about to read has been written by **Jane Richardson** who has been actively working in the industry for many years. Jane has been faced with many golden opportunities throughout her career, and as each one came along it pushed her higher up the ladder of success.

CHAPTER 23

Jane Richardson

This chapter has been written by Jane Richardson and it's about her inspirational journey in the beauty industry from how she started out as a new therapist straight from college to many years later becoming a top-class makeup artist and instructor for a large cosmetics company.

Becoming a Makeup Artist

I am in my classroom staring at a skull and sticks of coloured plasticine sitting in front of me on the bench. The room is unusually silent as our lecturer tells us that over the next week we are to build the muscles of the face, learning each one as we go. He goes on to explain that, once done, we are also to be tested on the various origins, insertions and facial expressions that each muscle makes. I am wondering where I am to start. I have no idea why I am doing this...

Twenty years later I am in a studio on London's south bank, staring at a skull, clay and modeling tools in front of me. I am on a three day Portraiture and Facial Anatomy Workshop studying the structure, planes, proportions and landmarks of the face. This time, I have an idea of where I am to start. I know exactly why I am doing this...

From the very beginning I had always wanted to work with makeup. My Mum had been an Avon lady when I was younger and both my sister and I used to love playing with all the makeup that she had, especially the tiny tubes of lipstick. At Secondary School I decided that I was to continue my studies at Chichester College of Technology and take the BTEC National Diploma Course in Beauty Therapy. My parents felt that I should go to college and complete 3 A levels first, and my Grandfather voiced his opinion saying that he thought only thick people studied Beauty Therapy. I was stubborn, the course was the equivalent of two A levels and that was all the reasoning I needed to go; and so it was that at age 16 that I found myself living in Chichester sharing an (often freezing) attic room with my new friend Claire who was studying Hairdressing and Beauty Therapy.

During my time spent in college I didn't immediately recognise my mentors who would somewhat influence my direction of growth; they tend to stand so quietly near to you, that often you nearly miss them. One of many has been my wonderful Beauty Lecturer whose creativity led her to one day decide to forgo the usual day makeup class and instead immerse her students in special effects. Learning how to create a wound was completely irrelevant to working in a salon as a therapist, but to some of us it was a true epiphany. That was the moment that made me realise that I'd fallen in love with the artistry. I wanted to be a makeup artist.

Drive, Ambition and Determination

My course was coming to an end and my family believed that I should stay on for another two years to do the BTEC Higher National Diploma. This course included more business studies and they felt that I would have more opportunities open to me on leaving. I had looked into makeup Schools but there weren't that many good ones around then and the ones that were good and established I couldn't afford. I remember talking to my mentor and voicing my concerns one day. I asked her if this was the only way I was to have any chance in the world or even to eventually run my own business if I enrolled on one of these courses. Her response was 'Jane, if YOU want a business, YOU will have a business, and you won't need this course to do it'. I didn't fully understand it then as I was too young to appreciate or even recognise my own strengths, but she had seen that I had drive, ambition and determination to succeed and believed I could do whatever I set my heart to.

Drive and determination is what you need in spades once you leave college. Most local salons were only hiring experienced Therapists and the salon where I had done work experience wanted me to work for less than what I should have been paid if I were a junior. So I decided to explore other avenues and I nervously walked in to my local leisure centre and asked to speak to the Manager there. Proposing that the facilities would be boosted by introducing a salon I was told that, whilst it was a good idea, there was no budget for it as an expensive extension had just been completed. I walked down the stairs only to turn around and go back up to ask for any job that they had. In my head, I thought I would be crazy to plant an idea and then walk away! I got a job on the reception desk, and then spent the next six months annoying the manager until she walked out one day with a cheque and proclaimed that we were going to set up the very first beauty salon in the Mid Sussex District Council Leisure Centre, and from the health suite offer Beauty treatments three days a week!

Some of your belief systems are not your own. My mother believes that I have 'weak ankles'. Now, I am sure that this was a protective belief to perhaps stop me doing things where I might hurt myself but my ankles are fine. When asked why she believed this it turns out she has no idea! Beliefs can be protective but they can also be limiting so it's wise to use them positively or to lose them completely! My Grandfather believed that only thick people studied to be Beauty Therapists and we all know that that is such a misconstrued belief, but a belief of his however from generations past. Everyone is entitled to their own opinion, including my own Grandfather, but I did not and do not believe this to be true, or else this belief could have stifled me, but instead I have used it (and indeed STILL use it) to drive me forward.

Specialising in a Different Niche

It was this drive that made me look at specialising. I wanted to do something that would perhaps set me apart from other Beauty Therapists and I particularly loved Massage so I decided to investigate this avenue further. It was something that I felt I was good at and it made sense to look into various options. Whilst looking at the courses offered at the then Clare Maxwell Hudson School of Massage I became interested in Manual Lymphatic Drainage.

Manual Lymph Drainage (MLD) uses the lightest of touch which takes time to master and so the training was split into four parts which included Basic, Therapy I, Therapy II and Therapy III. I was fascinated by the fact that this was a non-invasive technique that simply used the muscles and structure of the existing lymphatic's to clear accumulated fluid. When taken further it could ease swelling and inflammation and reduce pain caused by trauma from accidents or surgical intervention thereby speeding up the healing rate of damaged structures. I decided to do the basic course but found myself hooked once again in a completely new area so I signed up for the higher levels which focused on CDT (Complex (or combined) Decongestive Therapy). This would then allow me to treat Lymphedema and lipoedema and would take me to the Dr.Vodder School in Walchsee, Austria. It's here that I met the most amazing Therapists, two of whom Rachel and Adrian are still great friends to this day and had a life changing experience in one of the most incredible places I have ever been to. The last two levels were five days each, and covered various pathologies with an emphasis on lymphedema treatment. Theoretical instruction was given by the medical director alongside bandaging and specific MLD treatments. We had to take an oral, written and practical exam and whilst quite honestly this was the most stressful time of my life, it was also the most rewarding. I have memories from this time that I will cherish forever.

Acquiring a new skill set required me to re-evaluate what I was doing. I had invested a lot of my time and money on studying MLD and was now (at the age of 22) one of only thirty qualified practitioners in the UK. I started to discuss the possibility of setting up on my own with various people around me and through this discovered that one of the Instructors in the gym was thinking of doing the same. Again another chance conversation that would lead to a great opportunity. He was looking for space to set up a private gym and agreed to look for premises large enough to include me in the set up. Before long I gave up my job at the leisure centre and set up my own business, renting out one of the rooms on a full-time basis. I offered all the traditional Beauty Treatments alongside the MLD Therapy but soon discovered that whilst the location was great for my clients it was not suitable for my patients. Walking up stairs didn't always work, and the room being located directly opposite the reception desk just wasn't private enough for those with lymphedema wearing bandages. Something that I unfortunately overlooked at the time. Luckily, because the owner wanted a physio to be on site once a week to meet the demand, I was able to rent out my room to a physiotherapist from a local clinic. Through yet another conversation I found myself being offered two rooms in their clinic which was located on a quiet road with private parking. My time at the gym was over and I re-located to the clinic where I stayed for a number of years. Another opportunity came knocking on my door!

My Business Depends on Me

You need to care about both your clients *and* yourself to be a good therapist. Patience, empathy and heart are required as it doesn't matter whether you are waxing or doing a massage, you are transferring and receiving vast amounts of energy. I would often be half way through a treatment wondering where this blinding headache had come from or why I suddenly wanted to cry only to have my client burst into tears or get up and tell me that they had come in with a headache and that it was now gone. Taking time to recharge your own energy levels and taking care of your body is essential otherwise you will find yourself exhausted most of the time. I found myself suffering from Carpal Tunnel Syndrome and it was at the point where an operation was the only way to stop the pain. I had simply ignored the warning signs and continued to work even when suffering, but thankfully had a chiropractor that wasn't afraid to state the obvious by simply asking me "Why don't you just give up the massage?" My answer was to train as a Reflexologist as I thought maybe that would be better for me, but then still continued providing massage treatments! (not much of an answer). Most people go for the 'cure' option often ignoring the problem which is the very thing that is causing the pain. I knew I just couldn't give up as my clients and patients were relying on me, and what's more my business depended on me to be able to deliver all the treatments. Or so I thought...

Walking to work would quite often be my most favourite time of the day as this would provide me with a few minutes of calm, and precious time to process my thoughts. My home was only a ten-minute walk through a local park to my salon and on one particular morning I found myself walking to work in tears. The week had been a tough one. I had been called out to see a patient at home who had had his lymph nodes removed in his throat resulting in severe swelling of the head. He had been treated by a therapist from the local hospice but she was away and they needed me to step in. You never know quite what to expect but even as the nurse was gently preparing me for what I was to see (and smell) I would never in my wildest dreams have expected what I saw. I couldn't have imagined that the head could swell so much. They had tried surgically to help connect some lymph pathways by taking a skin graft from his leg and creating a 'sausage' shape that attached from the cheek to under his collar bone. His eyes were closed and bulging, his lips were swollen and his tongue was now so large it hung outside his mouth. I was told that he could hear me but of course could not see me or speak to me. I was nervous and honestly wondering what the hell I could do for him. The poor man had me waffling on in his ear for an hour and a half whilst I first cleared the pathways around his shoulders and chest and then worked on the skin graft and finally the eye area. I left the room and asked his fiancé if I could see a photo of him. I was presented with an image of a handsome young man full of life, completely unrecognisable from the man that I had just treated. She asked if I would be able to come back the next day and after making arrangements for a suitable time I went to the car...and cried. Later that night she called to tell me that they would be moving him to the hospice the next day and to ask if I would be able to see him there. She told me that normally after the treatment he could open his eye only a slither allowing him to talk by writing to her but this time his eye had opened completely and he could see her too! She was ecstatic as it allowed them to communicate better and I was choked. I will never forget walking in to the room and seeing him on that second day. His eye was wide open and he could see me, giving me a double thumbs up as I came in. I laughed as I told him how awful I had felt waffling on to him the day before and he sweetly told me that he had thought I was most amusing! The whole family were around him and there was so much love in that room it was incredible. Hospices are not the sad places that we think they are. All most of us really want is a chance to say goodbye to our loved ones (he sadly passed away that night). I am grateful for meeting him and proud to know that in some small way I was able to help him communicate with the people that he loved in his last hours.

More than anything that day, I walked away knowing that life is a blessing. I needed to take a break and I needed to finally follow my heart. Researching makeup schools in London, I found the Delamar Academy and dialed the number.

Time For a Change

Penny Delamar herself answered my call that day and recommended that I come along to her makeup training school and attend the evening classes once a week. She told me that I could start that very evening and I did something that I had never, ever done before... I cancelled my last two salon appointments and jumped straight onto a train and headed for London. Now, I had never been to London on my own and navigating my way round for the first time was a nerve wracking experience. To put this into perspective I was 25 years old and going the wrong way on the tube!

I settled in quite nicely at the Delamar Academy and found that sometimes things look different when you change perspective. Week after week I was being told by my teacher that what I was doing wasn't good enough and one of my biggest problems was the brows. It didn't matter how hard I tried I just couldn't do them right, until I changed how I saw them. For years I had been removing brows with tweezers or wax and was looking at what needed to be taken away and not what needed to be put in! This simple realisation changed everything, except I still got told that what I was doing still wasn't good enough That was it, I stormed out of the class and headed to the office where Penny was working. I remember her listening to me explain what had been happening and once finished she just sat back and smiled at me. I then realised that my teacher was behind me in the doorway and Penny (who knew exactly why) asked him to explain why he was always having a go at me. His reply was that "It was to get the 'therapist' out of me and that in order to survive in fashion you have to be able to take criticism and to not be so soft". He had been waiting for me to toughen up and stand up for myself. I can tell you today that you will never really take the 'therapist' out of me but I have learnt not to take things as personally. It was an important lesson and one that I am grateful to him for providing.

I did the evening course for just over a year whilst saving up to do the next course which was studying Fashion, TV, Theatre, Hair, Casualty and Prosthetics. I started my professional makeup career the day after I finished my course working on an Ad-campaign and I loved it! From that moment onwards my life completely changed and took on a new and exciting direction as I moved to London. I employed a therapist to work in the salon in my home-town during the week and I returned home each weekend to work there. At last it worked out that I didn't have to deliver all the treatments myself after all (the pain from Carpal Tunnel started to lessen) and the business no longer depended just on me to make it successful.

My next mentor came in the guise of a BAFTA Award winning makeup artist. She was a painter, a true artist, and someone who could see faces like no other. I learnt how to create characters and to use subtle makeup techniques to transform an actor into someone else. I remember creating a makeup one day for continuity using the Polaroid shot from the last scene as a reference. He had been splashed with paint and the actor was sitting patiently whilst I re-created each splash of paint, dot by dot, too perfection. The makeup designer came over and took one look at what I was doing and grabbed the brush from my hand. Picking up the paint she threw it at him a few times and handed me the brush back. It was TV, it was a small box , and it didn't have to be perfect. I was trying way too hard and a lesson was learnt! It was such an incredible experience and I was glad to have worked with her as the next shows' designer was someone that could have put me off working in television ever again.

I continued to work in television for about six years, and found it to be a great job but a hard one. You are the first in and the last to leave. I would be up around 4.30/5am and wouldn't arrive back home until 9pm. I often went to a photo shoot straight after finishing a night shoot and at the weekend I was back on a train and working in my salon. Amazing what you can do when you have to but something that I would eventually have to give up. I would never have been able to make the decision to close my business that I had spent so many years building up - but fortunately for me the universe delivered. The clinic wanted my rooms for a Pilates studio and I was given a months' notice. Relocating a business in a month just wasn't possible for me at the time and to be honest I was too tired to fight anymore. I was left with no choice but to close the salon completely. Saying goodbye to my clients and patients was tough as I felt like I was letting them down. I also felt like I was letting my parents down as yet again I was doing something they didn't agree with nor did they understand. I was convinced they must have thought I had lost it. Just giving up on it, moving full time to London was not something that was easy for them to comprehend. Sitting in the back of my parents car waiting for my Dad to lock up the factory where my equipment was going to be stored, my Mum simply said, "You never do anything the easy way do you?" Maybe she was right. All I know is that the very first Saturday that I didn't have to get on a train to come back home to work in my salon bought about a huge relief. That was when I realised that I had done exactly what I had done before – I'd focused so much on the job and the people around me that I hadn't taken care of myself and my needs. I had my weekends back and I so needed them.

Becoming a Great Sales Person

When not working on a TV show, my days would normally be filled with photo shoots but on one occasion I found myself in a quiet spell. Now I know that I needed to rest but this particular quiet spell was proving too long and was proving too much. I was driving my flat mates crazy by cleaning like a woman possessed and word soon got around that I was available for work. I found myself being asked if I would help on a counter as a freelance makeup artist for a cosmetics company. My initial answer to them was no. I had never wanted to work in store but in the end I was persuaded to help a friend out and so joined the team on the counter. I was conscientious, turned up on time, and applied good makeup. All good stuff I assumed, well at least I thought so? Funny how years later you look back and realise that you could have in fact done things better. I believe now that being a good retail makeup artist relies on you learning about sales, customer service and being able to teach people how to do it for themselves. I had had my own business and whilst my salon was booked up my sales sucked. I was so busy making sure they felt good as they were leaving I forgot to offer advice to them on products. I am not talking about hard sell here just the ability to communicate your professional opinion by recommending what they need. I was making a lot of money but looking back I could have been making a lot more. On the counter you need to be able to sell as well as apply a good makeup and to do both you have to listen to what the customer really wants and not be afraid of discussing products with them. It is a skill to be mastered and definitely something to be proud of.

Celebrating an event with the team one night I found myself talking to the CEO from the US. Two cocktails were pretty much all it took for me to verbally agree to work full time with the company. When I give a verbal agreement it seems that there is no going back (as far as I am concerned). I had been asked to consult on a counter and see if it was viable. Of course, my three months 'consulting' turned into two years as I was determined to prove that you could make a 1-5 customer a day account work. It can. With a whole lot of heart and great customer service it can work. There were days when I would wonder what I was doing and feel like I had gone backwards. I now realise it was just sideways; something to take me on a completely different path. There is never a straight and direct path to follow as your route can take you off in many sideways directions that will eventually steer you back to your destiny.

From this I went on to be a National Makeup Artist for the company, where I met my next great mentor Caroline, who then gave me a chance to work as a Training Manager for Europe. I couldn't have trained the staff if I hadn't have stood in their shoes and been there at the ground roots like they were. Not only had I been in the same position as them I had also worked on the counters at one of the quietest stores.

I love education. I love learning new skills personally and training other makeup artists to develop their own, helping them to understand what they are doing and how they can break it down to teach their customers. I went on to develop and strengthen my own learning further by studying profiling and to be an NLP Practitioner.

Whilst this was all great I found myself getting further and further away from what I really loved to do, my passion in makeup artistry. Working on strategy meetings, organising conferences and sticking to budgets were all great things to work on but something wasn't right. My body was trying to tell me (I started suffering from Anxiety attacks due to tiredness and stress and even developed Rosacea) but I wasn't listening.

I found myself being asked if I would consider taking on a new position back as an artist, representing the company on a higher level. It was a difficult decision. What about all the work I had put in over the last few years? What had been the point of it all? Thankfully my sister and my mentor helped me put it into perspective and make me realize that I would be happier. Change can be scary, and I won't lie, it was hard letting go of my old role. I love being back to my artistry full time, and am proud to be representing the company internationally working on photo shoots, backstage and on events. I have my brushes back in my hand and I am back to where my heart lies. I am proud that I am able to do the things that I can. Proud that I have many skills to pull on, and have experienced enough to be able to start mentoring others.

I love my job.

When you think you are going backwards you are not.

Study faces. Understand not just the skin but the bone structure.

Try not to worry about what other people think.

Never stop learning.

Jane Richardson

CHAPTER 24

Get a Life!

Keep On Moving On

If you have even the slightest thought of sitting back, through despondency or boredom, it's time to revisit your objectives as to why you're actually in business and give yourself a kick-start in the right direction to get yourself on track with this wonderful experience you're having being your own boss. Maybe you have a good solid base of clients now and are able to employ someone to help you service them on a part-time basis, maybe you need a virtual assistant to help you with the business administration or maybe it's time to start working ON your business a bit more rather than IN your business 24/7.

When all's said and done about making lists, putting effective plans in place and using every moment of your available time efficiently, your work/life balance is key to not only your business success but also your sanity (I do so hate that term work/life balance but I couldn't think of another one to replace it).

We all need to take a break at some time or another, and that may be just a few days doing nothing at all to a full two weeks away in the sun abroad. It's far too easy to become totally blinkered in our business life and taking time out just doesn't seem to happen often enough. We come up with excuses like "How will the business cope without me", "I'm not earning enough money so I can't really afford it" and "If I'm not around to take phone-calls I might miss some important client appointments". Let me tell you that your business *will* survive without you (or for a couple of weeks at least).

So as well as taking those well-earned breaks and holidays each year that you need in order to function more effectively, you should also be looking at things you can do on a daily basis during your working week to achieve improved results.

In order to perform better at work your mind, body and soul needs to be fit and healthy.

Mind – Feed you mind by reading an inspiring article or a chapter of a business book daily and this will make you feel motivated and enthused. Check out all the different types of wholesome foods that you can eat to help with your mental functions as well.

Body – You shouldn't sit in one position or stand for long lengths of time, so move around every forty-five minutes if you can. Adopt some simple arm and leg exercises into your working day to ease muscle fatigue and to get the blood flowing more effectively.

Since doing yoga I have found some great little exercises that are so quick and easy to do to help ease the stresses and the strains that build up during the day through either sitting in one place for too long or standing in one position for hours on end.

Soul – How about feeding your soul by doing something that is for you and only you, and in no way business driven. This can include relaxation, swimming, listening to music, going shopping, gardening, spending time with friends you don't see very often. Do something other than working in or on your business that makes you feel good leaving you with a feeling of accomplishment.

Oh, and don't forget to include all those mind, body and soul activities into your diary time sheets that we discussed earlier as well, along with all your short-breaks and holidays.

~~~~~

So we've covered quite a lot in this book and I really hope that you feel inspired by what you've read. Perhaps it has given you that much needed push and determination you longed for in order to organise your business ideas, your tasks and pending projects into a more realistic and categorised system so that you can work more productively with the hours that you have available to spend on business growth.

Maybe now you have a clearer picture on what it takes to actually meet the needs that your client has and how to be more benefit driven in providing a service that they actually want and *not what you think they want*. It could be the right time for you to think more about how you can build an ongoing relationship with them.

Hopefully I have shone some light onto the vast range of opportunities that you have at your fingertips to promote and advertise your business with regards to all of the proven marketing strategies that I have used successfully over the years and have possibly reduced any fears you may have had regarding marketing your hair or beauty business as a whole.

Let me know how you get on, I'm looking forward to hearing from you so please feel free to contact me anytime at sherrill@mimicks.co.uk

Our Home Site: www.mimicks.co.uk
Our Training Site: www.facepaintingtraining.com
Our Products Site: www.facepainting.uk.com

Sherrill Church

~~~~~~

ABOUT THE AUTHOR

Sherrill Church is the founder of Mimicks Face Painting, which was established in 1990. Over two decades later business is still booming and Sherrill is now painting 2nd generation customers and she enjoys a satisfying and very financially rewarding lifestyle that can only come from running a successful business that she is still passionately in love with.

Sherrill's year-round working weekends consist of providing creative make-up services such as face painting, glitter tattoos and henna body art at birthday parties, school fetes, community fun-days, and shows and festivals, and is very much in demand at company events for business promotion. Her daughter Ashlea Henson, who was a young child when she started the company, is now a partner in the business and is responsible for the creative side of the company.

During the week Sherrill trains those who are looking to start a face painting company and are in need of learning the basic skills to get them going. She is also a training provider for one of the large Hair and Beauty Wholesalers and her courses take her across the whole of the UK. She teaches at her local college as well, delivering subjects such as Makeup Artistry, Fashion and Photographic Makeup and Cosmetic Makeup. Recently she has been providing continued professional development courses for lecturers in colleges teaching them too on how to deliver the Themed Face Painting unit by City & Guilds and VTCT in their own colleges.

People often ask her about the accomplishment and longevity of her business and how come it's been so successful over the years. It really is quite simple she says – She just has full-on passion and a strong belief in what she does, loving every moment and living the life she loves!

Neither the author or publisher will accept responsibility for any damages or loss that may result from using the ideas, advice or any other information that has been outlined in this book. The outcomes may not be suitable for every situation nor for every person.

The author and publisher make no warranties with respect to accuracy nor suitability of the contents of the work herein and specifically disclaim all warranties of fitness for any particular purpose.

This book is sold on the understanding that neither the author or publisher has rendered full legal advice, accounting advice or service advice as the reader should seek further professional advice where applicable.

www.ingramcontent.com/pod-product-compliance
Lightning Source LLC
Chambersburg PA
CBHW071832270326
41929CB00013B/1969